BIBLICAL

LEADERSHIP

A CUT ABOVE

PRINCIPLES FOR

THE 21ST CENTURY

KYLE DODD

A Cut Above

Copyright © 2000 by Cross Training Publishing

Library of Congress Cataloging-in-Publication Data

ISBN 1-929478-12-7
Kyle Dodd

Distributed in the United States and Canada by Cross Training Publishing

For additional books and resources available
through Cross Training Publishing contact us at:

Cross Training Publishing
P.O. Box 1541
Grand Island, NE 68802
(308) 384-5762
www.crosstrainingpublishing.com

CONTENTS

Foreword   7
Acknowledgments   9
Introduction   11

1. Standing Alone under Enemy Fire   13
2. Unity Not Union   19
3. Passivity   23
4. Servant Leadership   27
5. Leadership 101   33
6. Pride   37
7. Joy and Laughter   41
8. Personal Disciplines   45
9. Your Calling   51
10. Empowerment   55
11. Success   59
12. Re-solving Conflict   63
13. Stamina   67
14. Art of Communication   71
15. Art of Listening   77
16. Casting Vision   81
17. Imagination   85
18. Integrity   89
19. Handling Stress   93
20. Synergy   97
21. Choosing Your Mountains   101
22. Solitude   105
23. Crisis   109
24. Significance   113
25. Mentoring   117
26. Accountability   123
27. Money and Materialism   127

28. Core Values   131
29. Personal Growth   135
30. Failure   139
31. Charisma   143
32. Time Management   147
33. Effective Teaching   151

FOREWORD

Kyle is a gifted writer and communicator who knows the REAL needs of people. As a leader, you will benefit personally from *A Cut Above* because his writing is a merger of the truth of Scripture applied to the issues you and I face every day.

Dennis Rainey
Executive Director of FamilyLife Ministries
in association with Campus Crusade for Christ

ACKNOWLEDGEMENTS

I would like to dedicate this book to those in my life who have modeled the chapters in this book to myself and many others in this world. Their impact is immeasurable:

Sharon Dodd- my bride who has amazing stamina as a wife and mother.

Bo Snowden- high school coach who lead by example.

Jimmy Greenwood- huntin' partner who modeled integrity to his grave.

Bruce Morgan- peer who exemplifies empowerment.

Dr. Jim Dixon- pastor who shows others from where your significance should come.

Carl Dodd- my dad who modeled the value of hard work.

Debbie-Jo White- friend who knows her Godly calling.

Bob Hudson- father-in-law who models Christ-like values to my sons.

Dave Bliss- college coach that maintained unity.

Bo Mitchell- golf buddy who produces joy in others.

Kris Cooper- brethren who models servant leadership to thousands.

Bill Darrough- ministry and business partner whose priorities are to be admired.

Dennis and Barbara Rainey- fellow communicators with a proactive vision for marriage and the family.

Stan Holmes- accountability partner who listens first.

Joe White- past boss whose imagination is unbridled.

Dr. Danny Carroll- seminary professor who teaches

me the depth and meaning of the scriptures.

Dean Macfarlan- buddy that keeps biblical perspective during success.

Ken Roberts- friend and inner city pastor that slighted pride.

Chuck Kovac- new friend who showed a community how temporary crisis can have eternal rewards.

Lyle Sankey- rodeo buddy that taught me to laugh at life.

Kevin Whitley- pal that shows me parenting isn't passive.

Tim Brassfield- college bud that defined humility.

John Kriz- friend that spurs others to excellence.

Aaron Fleming- high school mentor who saw my potential.

Bob Howey- my mentor who models the importance of solitude.

Tom Parr-brother in Christ that facilitates synergy.

Keith Chancey- workout buddy with endless charisma.

Tommy Fergason- fellow camp director that operates in his gifting.

Bob Lepine- comrade whose values determine his priorities.

Scott Smith- high school teammate with incredible personal discipline.

Trent Ballard- companion with Divine security.

Steve Schall- friend with a kingdom vision.

Tom Dabasinskas- a yoke-fellow whose leadership is unsurpassed.

"Remember those who lead you, who spoke the word of God to you; and considering the result of their conduct, imitate their faith" Hebrews 13:7.

INTRODUCTION

As we enter the 21st Century and the new Millennium, if you are like most people in today's complex, fast-paced society, you sense a desperate need for a relevant and competent role model of effective leadership. In our world of media made celebrities there are few character created hero's in earth-suits to pattern our lives after. You long for some true standard of excellence and rightness in leadership.

I truly believe there is a perfect practitioner and teacher of leadership. That person is Jesus Christ who modeled the heart and methods of servant-leadership. I believe that in the infallible Holy Scriptures lies the encyclopedia for effective leadership.

People are looking for practical advice and applicable principles on leadership, yet rarely do they give serious consideration to God's Word for the answers. This is true of people from differing religions and beliefs as well as followers of Christ. Whichever the case, Jesus is not thought of nor His word as a relevant source or teacher of the how-to's on directing, inspiring, and equipping others for success.

In this book, I invite students of leadership from all backgrounds, cultures, race, and gender to join me as we take another look at the Bible and the genius methods of Jesus. In only three short years he demonstrated a radical form of leadership that created spectacular results with ordinary people and transformed the course of human history. By presenting this message of teamwork, character, sound method, and consistent behavior, I hope through the Bible and Holy Spirits impact, to bring NEW hope to a world in frantic need of a leadership revival.

1

Standing Alone under Enemy Fire

Hollywood in past years has brought it back to the public memory, but to those who were personally involved, it's still as real today as it was on June 4, 1944 in an operation code-named, "Overlord." Allied armies, with over 100,000 U.S., British and Canadian troops landed at dawn on the Normandy Coast in northern France. The bone chilling orders came down from Gen. Eisenhower, the supreme commander in Europe: "You are about to embark upon the Great Crusade, toward which we have striven these many months. The eyes of the world are upon you. The hopes and prayers of liberty-loving people everywhere march with you. Your task will not be an easy one. Your enemy is well-trained, well-equipped and battle-hardened. He will fight savagely." First, the 101st and 82nd airborne had landed behind the coastal defenses and had taken 2890 prisoners and were covering for the ground troops before they stormed the beach in boats called L.C.V.P.s-Landing Craft Vehicle Personal or as naval officers called it, Higgins boats.

A young soldier named Scott Pendleton Collins was one of those brave men who departed on their L.C.V.P. in the middle of the night from a battleship named, *The Jefferson,* destination code-named, "Omaha." Before their deployment, the naval chaplain had services and said, "Some of us won't be coming back" then he offered up a prayer for the soldiers' souls. Scott was told on the L. C. V. P. that his platoon was supposed to get on the beach, take care of the enemy, then follow the armored guys through this ravine to a place called: Vierville-sur-Mer. Omaha Beach, unknown to Scott at the time, was the place the most serious fighting from the enemy would take place and leave more than 3000 Allied casualties. The sea was choppy and tossing everyone in the boat around to the point of sickness. It was like the worst thunderstorm you'd ever seen or heard, but instead of being up in the sky it was on top of you. Omaha Beach was covered in smoke and haze, shells hissing overhead, great "booms" along the shore where the Navy was pounding enemy positions with bombs. The front ramp of the boat dropped abruptly, "Out of the boat! Out of the boat!" yelled Captain Zappacosta. Scott was scared to death and ashamed of being so scared yet he jumped over the side of the boat into about four feet of water equipped with his M-1. "Get to the beach!" the Captain ordered. Everything was in a panic yet Scott kept going under heavy enemy fire toward the beach that looked a thousand miles away. The water was filling up his boots and the sandy seafloor slipped beneath his boots. He could see guys falling all around him as they took hits from enemy fire. Scott knew when a fellow soldier had been shot by the way he jerked when the bullets hit him. Scott was moving toward big iron structures, which stuck up out of the shallow water where guys were crouched down together for safety. Scott finally fell behind a barricade, and when he did, bullets hit the sand right in front of him. A fellow soldier grabbed his shirt and pulled him to his feet as they started running toward the wall, yet whomever it was that helped him didn't make it. Scott got to the wall, turned and looked back on where he had been to see soldiers lying all over the beach either dead or critically wounded. He had made it to the checkpoint that commanding officer Lieut. Rowe had instructed him to; yet he was the only one who had made it safely out of his platoon. To his surprise he found himself standing alone.

Scripture brings to account another brave, saintly soldier who stood single-handedly against an enemy of 400. We read this in 1 Kings 22 about a leader of conviction and boundaries named Micaiah son of Imlah. There had been peace in the Middle East for the past three years until Ahab, King of Israel, called a meeting with Jehoshaphat, King of Judah, to consider a tag team against the Syrian army over the Omaha Beach of their day, Ramoth Gilead. Ahab was ready to go and storm the beach in light of the well trained, equipped, and battle hardened soldiers of opposition until Jehoshaphat thought it wise to seek counsel from Ahab's 400 prophets on payroll whose advice was tainted in truth. Their counsel... "Go, for the Lord will give land into your hands." The King of Judah asked if there was but one prophet who would speak differently. Yes there was and his name was Micaiah, who evidently had a bad past of differing views with his boss Ahab. He was immediately summoned, and en route, made well aware by one of the, "puppet prophets" that should he choose to differ his counsel which was not to deploy the troops, he would be standing alone. Micaiah obeyed his convictions and conscience and spoke nothing but truth in the midst of lies to the kings. After being verbally whipped by Ahab, Micaiah was slapped and sent to jail to be feed nothing but bread and water until the king's, "supposed" victorious, return.

The plot thickens here with Ahab switching uniforms with Jehoshaphat to deceitfully widen the target on his allies back and off they went into battle discarding the truth spoken from one lone soldier. As true prophecy proves, along with some righteous humor, in battle a random arrow was shot by enemy fire and ironically hit King Ahab between the vulnerable creases of his armor resulting in a fatal war wound. The king was propped up in his chariot so he could see first hand the consequences of his disobedience until he died that evening watching his troops' cowardly retreat with their tails tucked between their armor.

The legacy of disobedience continued in the gene pool to Ahab's son, Ahaziah as he continued doing evil in the eyes of the Lord and provoked God to righteous anger by his deeds and leadership styles, just as his father had modeled.

An unchanging Word in a changing world should give leaders a security in their tasks. In today's culture where politicians say whatever it takes to win votes, Godly leadership relies on scriptural standards as the barometer for the decision making process. Godly leadership means seeing the big picture of eternity in the midst of what seems to be an unwinnable war. Spiritual leaders realize that it is better to be divided by truth than united in a compromise. They consistently speak truth that heals rather than lies that destroy. It's a daily decision a Godly leader makes that it is better to be hated for telling the truth than to be loved and embraced for telling a lie. They see the value in standing alone for a righteous cause than to win with the multitudes. They recall the story of Noah and the Ark and remember that Noah went into the boat a minority and came out a majority. Effective leadership is the realization that in the long haul, it is better to ultimately succeed with the truth than temporarily succeed with a lie. It means standing alone, at times, and being mocked and tongue slapped for your standards. The sobering difference between bad leadership and the good type is that the results are polar.

There have been, and always will be, times in a godly leader's life where decisions of popularity vs. isolation seem inevitable. There is an old saying, "the higher the monkey climbs in the tree, the more of his rear you can see." Leadership positions are not for those who are not battle hardened from maintaining their convictions in midst of heated wars. There have been and always will be casualties and war. There's no difference in leadership. Whether you lead your family, company or a ministry, the best leaders train daily in truth and are well equipped with their helmet of salvation, breastplate of righteousness, firmly rooted in the infallible Word of God, outfitted with child-like faith and the Sword of the Holy Spirit. You realized early on in battle, the opposition isn't against flesh and blood but against evil powers of darkness. You believe this is a world war and you're not just playing army. Our Omaha Beach as a believer has already been won yet it's our daily battles of dying to self and avoiding the snares of the enemy that produce the successful fruit. You must be Spirit-lead to claim daily victory in the battles of the flesh. Perseverance and endurance throughout your journey is key to a victorious life on this earth. Opposition is by divine design to keep the spiritual soldiers from becoming dependent upon their personality and giftedness and promotes a daily ritual of interdependence with the Jesus Christ. Onward Christian soldier!

2

Unity Not Union

The year was 1979, the basketball team was the University of Oklahoma and we were headed to the "Big Dance" better known as the NCAA Basketball Championships for the first time in 40 years. We were a bunch of middle-class, very average ball players assembled from Indiana to Florida now residing in Norman, Oklahoma with head coach Dave Bliss. We had beaten Kansas State University for the Big 8 Conference title and now off to the post-season tournament in Kansas City. We made it to the finals of the post-season tournament to face the University of Kansas, which we defeated easily. We then got the big invite to the NCAA Tourney in the Midwest Regional bracket at a #5 seed to be matched up to play #4 seeded University of Texas in Dallas. After a substantial victory, we were off to the, "Sweet 16" and Cincinnati, Ohio to play #1 seeded Indiana State with All-American Larry Bird at the helm. Michigan State with star Magic Johnson and Indiana State with Larry Bird went on to clash in the NCAA Championship game. Michigan State stood victorious after the dust settled on the hardwood that night of March 26, 1979 in Salt Lake City. What a season and what an experience.

The part of the story that you don't know about was the adversity that was overcome all season long and the "Teamwork" that was maintained by coach Bliss as we dealt with emotional and physical problems throughout the successful season. Starting players going down with sprained ankles, a broken foot, and dislocated elbows. Petty jealousies arose over starting spots and playing time. The mark of a good leader isn't keeping the team going in the midst of victories but in the midst of chaos and disasters. The capability of keeping everyone's spirits up and their chins high when facing trials is a developed gift. Oklahoma had no business being one of the top 16 teams in the country yet we were. This team was deeply unified in purpose and intent.

Whether you're a coach, father, president, pastor, husband, or manager, one of the major functions of a successful leader is the ability to maintain not create "unity." Before we delve headfirst into the art of unity we first need to look at the leadership manual we call scripture. *Ecumenical* comes from the Greek word *oikumene* which meant "the entire inhabited world." Ephesians 4: 3 says, "Being diligent to persevere the unity of the Spirit in the bond of peace," Paul says to the church, team, family or business that unity is needed in order for survival. Eager is too mild a translation; it means be pro-active, aggressive in action to maintain unity!

When the "body" unites, it fulfills a prayer of Jesus in John 17:21, "That they may all be one; even as thou, Father, art in Me, and I in Thee, that they also may be in Us; that the world may believe that Thou didst send me." Jesus' desire is that all believers belong to the same household of God and should be visibly expressed in the exercise of exhortation through each other's differences. There is power in numbers and if we as believers can unite all of our different factions into one single Christian force, we can influence society in a major way.

In the "True" church of Christ, people gather at the same footing whether there are differences in income, color, and gender, Jew or Gentile without favoritism or distinction [1 Cor.12:13; Gal. 3:28; Col.3:11; James 2:1-6]. We don't ignore differences easily in our western culture! Friction has existed in the church and on this planet ever since the first Century between the Jews and Gentiles (Acts 15).

This old poem says it best:
To dwell above with the saints we love,
Oh that will be glory.
But live below, with saints we know—
Well, that's another story!

Ecumenicals try to manufacture a semblance of unity. Not the true unity of the Spirit, but a "union" of Christians. Union is an institutional, worldly entity. Unity is what God produces and we maintain. That's why Paul goes to the effort to not be misunderstood of where unity comes in Eph.4: 4-6. The church is a conglomeration of individuals who happen to agree on the same ideas. The idea of a body is that it consists of thousands of cells with one mutually shared life (Phil 2:9-11).

How do we get this "Unity" to maintain? Lets take a look at how the human body functions and see if we as leaders can glean any insights. The human body is formed by the growth and multiplication of many cells from one original cell. The body grows cell-by-cell until a mature body is formed. The secret…all parts of the body share life together. God's program for reaching and healing a broken world has always involved incarnation, which means, "to take bodily form." We as families, businesses, ministries, teams, are to function as a well-oiled machine with multiple parts doing what they were created to do, function together. Today, the body of Christ performs the work around the clock, around the globe for Christ. Corporately comprised of millions of cells [believers] on the same mission. Unity is a necessity for survival not only as a family, company, team, and staff but also as a body of believers. Seek to be unified not unionized!

3

Passivity

As fallen people, we all are guilty before God because of our sin nature (Rom. 3:23). As a leader, YOU are more responsible before God for your conduct, actions and the choices you make as you lead. Even in a world that consistently broadcasts the message that character doesn't count and can be separated, scripture objects. Lets take an example out of the Bible, beginning in the book of World Records (Genesis 3) and revisit the Garden of Eden. Adam has just been created from dirt and Eve is coming from the rib as Adam naps. Adam receives instruction and a job in his domain and soon watches a [crafty] snake smooth talk his wife into committing suicide while he stands passively by watching the story, plot, villain and climax unfold before his eyes while he said or did nothing (Gen. 3:6).

One of the biggest problems in our country today with leaders is the terminal disease of passivity. Leaders living lives of quiet desperation while sin manifests itself right before their eyes and they do nothing. I was in Anchorage Alaska and saw a sign outside the city limits on the way to Nome that read, "Choose your rut; you'll be in it for the next 1040 miles." What does it take to "jar" you out of your rut of passivity into action for the cause of Christ?

King David as a leader of Israel, father and husband to many, made some bad decisions by not making a decision at all. In 2 Samuel 24 you come upon a scene where God gives David a decision that will affect not only himself, but also his people. The Lord said, "I offer you three things; choose for yourself one of them, which I may do to you." The choices where: Door #1, seven years of famine on your land. Door #2, to run from your enemies for three days while they pursue you. Door #3, three days of plague in your land. Now I'm no rocket scientist but I think I know what would be the best decision here both for my people and myself. David chose door #3 and 70,000 people from the communities of Dan to Beersheba died just as the Lord had said. What? And you chose that option because? David knew from past experience that God was more merciful than men so he chose the third option, no matter whom it affected. Not to judge, but can you smell the scent of selfishness and self-concern in this story? Do you see the theme, "Looking out for #1" and how it takes precedence in the thought process?

Another sad story in the life of David comes in being an active father to his two sons and virgin daughter in 2 Samuel 13. One of his sons named Amnon falls in love with his sister Tamar and negotiates a plot with his misfit buddy Jonadab the son of Shimeah [David's brother] to rape his sister via a carefully planned set-up. The irony of Tamar's dress [a sign of virginity] should touch your heart. She was the daughter of a King, staying pure, waiting for her "Knight In Shining Armor." The robe she wore as she was raped was her cloak of honor and dignity. Amnon was David's first born son. His name meant, "trustworthy" and "faithful" which he was not. Amnon simply grew up watching his dad take one wife after another in a land where polygamy was forbidden. His father got everything he wanted like a spoiled child. Bathsheba and Tamar were both described by the same adjective, "Beautiful" in 2 Sam. 11:2 and 13:1. Amnon called his personal servant [even though he knew the servant would talk] and did everything to disgrace Tamar's feeling of shame. Tamar lived the rest of her life in desolation and disgrace. Both Absalom and David reacted to the situation wrongly in more than one way. In your words, what was Absalom telling Tamar to do when he said, "be quiet" and "take this thing to heart?"

David's next words: "Show me, Lord" in Ps.39: 4 is him pouring out his heart to God for guidance. Absalom asked Tamar to live with him but she was not invited to be honest about her feelings. David knew of the lack of character in Amnon year's prior, yet passivity caused him to do nothing before disaster struck.

David needed to apply the wisdom in Ps.39 yet even after the event, he did nothing and remained passive. David didn't take control of the family tragedy. Satan was using the "sin of failure" to completely disable him. Restoration doesn't mean you can no longer stand for the truth because you fell! Restoration means you MUST Stand! David allowed his failure and un-involvement to stop him from leading his household in justice and righteousness.

Leaders lead by the Spirit of God and have got to develop their "big picture" perspective of situations through a divine touch. What I mean by that is exactly what the prophet Isaiah admonished us to do, "Mount up with wings like eagles" (Is. 40:31) and see things from God's point of view. One of the greatest quotes for leadership that has stuck with me for a lot of years is, "You make your decisions and then, your decisions will make you." Spiritual leadership isn't shooting from the hip when making decisions; it's being intentional and purposeful.

You, as a leader, can't change the past but you can darn sure learn from it and change some things so the legacy of sin doesn't flow to another generation. One of the lamest excuses of a leader is, "That's the way I was taught or trained" or "That's how I was raised." God created anger to energize us to respond when something is wrong! David needed to channel his anger and respond to the crime committed in his family. No weaker household exists than the one that lacks active AUTHORITY. Lack of it is a breeding arena for reckless sin and behavior that damages not only you, but also those around you...just ask David and his daughter Tamar.

4

Servant Leadership

One of the gifts of the Spirit as expressed in I Corinthians 9 is the gift of leadership or ruling. The Greek translates the word to mean: One who stands in front. The world's view of leadership and authority places someone over someone else, as in a military command structure, a business executive hierarchy, or a governmental system. This system is urged on by competitiveness, the fall of the human race, and faced with rebelliousness and ruthlessness of a sinful human nature. The world as we know it today would not function without the use of command structures and executive decision-making. Jesus was quick to point out that, "It shall not be so among you." Believers are in different relations to one another than is the world. We as Christians are brothers and sisters, children of one Father. Jesus put it plainly in Matthew 23:8, "You have one teacher, and you are all brethren." Throughout the centuries, we have ignored the words of Christ and repeatedly borrowed the authority and leadership structures of the world, changed the names from kings, generals, governors, secretaries, captains, presidents and chiefs to popes, patriarchs, bishops, stewards, deacons, pastors and elders and gone on our merry way. Leaders are not to exercise their authority as bosses but as examples! When they themselves obey the Word, others will be motivated to follow. The influence of a servant-leader is not the power to give orders but the ability to inspire enthusiasm and voluntary cooperation. God never forces our obedience, He attracts our devotion and love-and he does it by awakening in us our gratitude and our responsiveness to His love. "We love, because He first loved us" (1 John 4:19).

Jesus was on his way to Jerusalem (Matt. 19:28) to suffer on the cross when he decided to stop and teach an important lesson to his band of disciples (Matthew 20:20-28). James and John got their mother to petition for them the place of power at the "Right hand of the throne of God." Jesus never rebukes them for, "Wishing" to be great and successful but tells them in simple terms that they must go up the ladder as He came down (Phil 2:1-6). You would think after this lesson on climbing the ladder of success that the disciples would have gotten the message. A few days later at a Passover meal, the practicality of the message is at hand as the guests arrive and the youngest or least ranked invitee amongst the disciples failed to seize the opportunity to serve as a foot washer for dirty feet as the guests entered the house for the Passover meal (John 13:1-27). As one might expect, Jesus the Messiah, would gird his loins and stoop from being a king to being a, "Doulos" [bond-servant]. Jesus showed his motley crew by service, exactly what He meant by, "The Least shall be first and the first shall be last."

In this story, old peppermint socks Peter [always had his feet in his mouth] doesn't comprehend the lesson at hand and rebukes Jesus for his act (John 13:10). The point was that Jesus didn't quit being God to be a servant; you're seeing, "Deity" in a towel, washing feet! The lesson Jesus wanted his men to catch here was that servanthood isn't sitting around a table talking theology, it's doing it. Serving someone else is right at the heart of the message of the cross and Calvary whether you like them or not. Doing something for someone who doesn't deserve or expect the sacrificial act is supernatural. You must have your security and self-worth absorbed in your spiritually identity.

We need to stop focusing so much on the throne and positions of power and more on the job at hand. The higher a man climbs in his field the greater the problems. Despite what our world promotes as the secrets of success, we must realize only God promotes and He is only going to promote servants. The world says to do whatever it takes by, lying, cheating, self-promotion, or gossip and this is a means to getting to the top. God's Word teaches to the contrary. The ironic scenario is that we all want to be a servant until we are treated as such. A great quote I once heard says, "Why stoop to be a king when you can be a servant."

Here are just a few guidelines to help you in your acts of service:

Servant leaders have a unique ability to see practical needs and have a burden of heart to meet them (Phil. 2:20).

Servant leaders have a special enjoyment in providing for physical needs that comfort (2 Tim. 4:13).

Servant leaders long to be with others in order to serve them (Acts 6:2; 17:14-15).

Servant leaders have a tendency to feel inadequate and unqualified for spiritual leadership when how they serve is Jesus' main way of communicating commitment and love (1 Tim. 4:14; 2 Tim. 3:10-14).

Servant leaders don't mind being treated as a servants. They see this as an opportunity to use their gift and exhort others to utilize their own gifts (Phil 2:22).

Servant leaders don't just serve those they like. They serve those who have needs.

Servant leaders are secure, knowing God values them.

Servant leaders are high on relationships and low on control and coercion.

Servant leaders shun the trappings of authority and status.

Servant leaders base their authority on character, not on the position they occupy.

Leadership, God's style, always looks like a servant stooping to the task at hand. Leadership is not about pleasing everyone else but pleasing just ONE. Biblical leadership is NOT sitting on your throne bossing others around like they are peasants to meet your every need. If you're apart of a family, team, company, school or whatever arena you're in, you are called to exemplify Christ by serving. A little side note here is needed. Don't choose those you want to serve by what they can give in return or who might notice your humble act. The act dictates who you serve, not the person or reward. During the Passover meal, remember, Jesus served the very man Judas who would sell out his commitment for a measly $40.00 and he still got his feet washed by the Master despite His knowing the betrayal would happen. Mother Teresa once said, "We are called to obedience, not to success." In the Bible leaders are servants, both of God and His people. As a leader, you truly are the least of all the saints. Remember, a servant's heart is not a part of the original equipment, it's an upgrade!

5

Leadership 101

The Bible is full of people who were positioned in strategic leadership roles. Their styles cover a variety of ranges: Nehemiah the Planner, Peter the Impetus, Jethro the Management consultant, Lydia the House Church Leader.

In the book of Nehemiah you will find valuable illustrations and characteristics portrayed in the life and actions of Nehemiah as he takes on the God-size task of rebuilding the wall around Jerusalem. Let's take a contrasting look at leadership characteristics and Nehemiah illustrations portrayed in scripture in 445 B.C. First, a little background is needed to set the stage. Nehemiah was a man of great character and was a Jew living in Persia at the time as a cupbearer [one who checks the wine for poison before the king drinks and is very loyal] for the pagan King Artaxerxes. Jerusalem at this point was defense-less, wall-less and vulnerable to a pagan culture yet Nehemiah hears a call to the wall in this holy city. Nehemiah begins his mission in April 446 B.C. by praying for four months. The King grants Nehemiah a passport for travel and timber for supplies from Asaph.

He makes a secret ride around the city and assembles Judah's leaders and shares his burden for the wall and the people it surrounds. Let us glean some Biblical wisdom from Nehemiah and what he encountered as a leader:

Let me preface all this data with a fact. Leadership and management are very different. I do think they go together like salt and pepper but the fact remains, they're different in styles and functionality. Leaders have a knack to visualize the final result of a major undertaking like building a wall around a holy city. Nehemiah visualized the goal of removing the "great affliction and reproach" of God's people by rebuilding the wall (Neh.1:2-3).

Leaders have ability to breakdown major goals into smaller, more achievable tasks. Nehemiah accomplished the huge effort of rebuilding the wall by having lots of groups working on small sections of the project (Neh. 3:1-32).

Leaders have the ability to know what resources are available and needed to reach a common goal. Leaders are not afraid to make bold, "Asks." Look how Nehemiah requested from the pagan king the resources to rebuild the wall: a certain time, letters of introduction, safe escorted travel and lumber (Neh. 2:6-8). Nehemiah is a man of great wisdom knowing what he wants and when he wanted it.

A Godly leader has a tendency to remove himself from the spot-lite and distracting details in order to focus on the big picture and ultimate goal. Nehemiah wasn't involved in the building itself but removed obstacles that would hinder the workers such as financial pressures (Neh. 5:1-13).

A leader has a willingness to endure reaction from insiders and outsiders to reach an ultimate goal. Nehemiah had opposition from within and without in his efforts to rebuild the wall (Neh. 4:8-18).

Most aggressive leaders of today have a need for loyalty and confidence from those who are being directed and served. Nehemiah brought a great assembly of people against the nobles and routers to discourage the people. He required oaths of cooperation from them also.

Leaders have a unique ability to know what they should and should not delegate to others. Nehemiah delegated the work on the walls, but he retained the responsibility of dealing with enemies and guarding the walls (Neh.4:13).

Leaders have the ability to inspire and encourage workers by cheerfulness, approval, praise, and challenging them beyond their own efforts. Nehemiah is about building into people, not just finishing a project. Nehemiah had a cheerful spirit (Neh.2:1). He was skillful and challenging and encouraging and caring beyond the task when it came to his fellow teammates (Neh.4:14).

To a leader there is no greater joy or fulfillment than seeing all the parts come together in a finished product. Nehemiah expressed his joy in the completed task by appointing singers and uniting the people in a revival and celebration (Neh. 7:1-2 and 8:1-18).

A few warnings for those that lead: James 3:1 says, "Let not many of you be leaders because you know that we who lead will be judged more strictly." In the scriptures, we are ALL guilty before God but leaders are more responsible to God.

There are times when the position of leadership begins viewing people as human resources rather than as human beings. Leaders may have a tendency to use people to accomplish personal ambitions rather than build the kingdom for God. At times, you'll find leaders showing favoritism to those who appeared to be more loyal or responsive to requests than the rest. You see this at times in large families showing favoritism to one child over another. Leaders fail when they take charge of projects, which were not in God's plan. Some leaders become so consumed with their power they forget their servanthood calling and delegate too much work to others to free up their own schedule for fun. Some leaders tend to avoid constructive confrontation and overlook serious character flaws in valuable family members, co-workers, teammates, and staff members because it may hinder the cause or outcome of the project. Being unresponsive to suggestions and appeals is a sure fire way of getting yourself into hot water. An unexamined or unchallenged life leads to the deadly trap of self-satisfaction and apathy.

Let me close this chapter out by saying that along the way, you as a leader can value others by giving them proper explanations and praise as fellow teammates and future heirs to the kingdom. There is nothing worse than being in the lead and not knowing where you are going. When a leader, you are apart of the "Sin" of your people, not just fixing it. Nehemiah instructed [Hebrew word meaning to cause understanding] his people and led them out of their sin through repentance. There are two things that will last forever, people and God's word, not projects!

6

Pride

Was pride the first sin? You read Isaiah 14:12-14 and Genesis 3:1-6 and draw out your own conclusion. There are two kinds of pride in our fallen world: Inflated and deflated. Inflated- I feel I am better than the world around me. I am also constantly seeking to push myself ahead and am never satisfied with the way God has made me. Deflated- I focus on my weaknesses, shortcomings, and inadequacies. This is a negative manifestation of pride [kind of pride in reverse], but I am still dissatisfied with the way God has made me. So what common thread is in both kinds of pride?

The strange thing about pride is how we manifest it. We can do this in many ways beginning with an unforgiving spirit [Matt.6:14-15]. This rears its ugly head when we see ourselves as better than most and become judicial judges in the kings court. You see this a lot in marriages and among friends when they feel like their "rights" have been violated and their feelings are hurt. "Surrender" in the true meaning of the Greek New Testament looks like: hands extended, palms up to be handcuffed, under authority with no rights. Grace comes into play because most who don't forgive don't understand the unmerited favor God has extended to them. Do you hurt God by your disobedient actions or words? Does God forgive you (Matt. 6:14-15)?

We obtain pride by trying to "save face" (Matt.5:23-24) in circumstance in which we feel we are going to lose it. We have pride in our socioeconomic status as declared in Luke 12:15. When we are self-righteous and holier than thou (Ecc. 7:16) or when it comes to how we handle authority in Matthew 20:25-27. What does this pride cost me? It can cost you the destruction of your family, business or team (Prov. 16:18-19). You will encounter shame and rejection not only internally but also externally (Prov. 11:2 and 1 Pet. 5:5). To boil it down for you, pride is destructive because it is a wall between you and your relationship with Christ. Why? It means I am not letting God have total control of my life.

God's definition looks like this: Man exalts himself–God humbles man. Man humbles himself–God exalts. E.G.O is when we edge God out of our lives and circumstances. God's solution to this solvable challenge is humility. During Pharaoh's reign, there was a harness that yoked two stallion chariot horses together that pulled the Ruler called a "Humility harness." Its purpose was not to take the stallions high-spirited nature out of the horse but to get the energy and purpose moving together in the same direction. When I think of humility in an earth-suit I think of my dad who lives this out daily. He was the starting quarterback of the longest winning streak [47 wins and1 loss] in the history of Division I football at the University of Oklahoma under the coaching of Bud

Wilkinson. This team won two national championships from 1954-1958. I have never heard my dad brag or boast about his personal athletic achievements that still stand today in the record books. Humility is not thinking less of yourself but thinking of yourself less. Humility is not thinking too highly or too lowly of yourself. It's accepting God's plan with gratitude and thankfulness and giving Him all the Glory in the process. It understands God is in control [which takes faith] and willingly trusts Him to work out any circumstance or situation that might arise. Don't trust your gifts, success, education [in our country today, we are educated beyond our intelligence] or experience…. trust God!!!

So how do you deal with pride? First, you ask God to make you aware of any prideful areas in your life. Second, you see yourself from God's perspective (John 15:5-6). Third, you focus on God's power when you pray and praise Him (Acts 17:28). Last, you follow Christ's example (Phil. 2:5-11). Humility really is pride under submission. When E.G.O. is involved, the way we evaluate someone is by external rewards, not internal peace. People are going to put you on a pedestal as a leader; YOU have to remove yourself from it!

7

Joy and Laughter

The Bible teaches us that joy and laughter are, "Good medicine for the soul" (Prov. 17: 22). Laughter is a gift God has given to us all to help take the lumps of life. The medical field shows that it takes twice as many muscles in your face to frown as it does to smile. So why is everyone frowning? Did you know that smiling is as contagious as the chicken pox? Try it some time at a stoplight, look over at the person in the car next to you and smile. They will smile back wondering what your up to.

I have surrounded myself with optimistic people who love to laugh as a by-product of internal joy. We laugh at jokes [clean ones I might add], life, and we've learned to laugh at ourselves. When you stop laughing you've got a joy problem. I'm not saying that you should go around laughing at everything that moves, but I do think laughter eases the tension life strangles you with and produces a more optimistic attitude. One of the fruits of the Spirit is joy (Gal. 5: 22). The most effective communication includes an emotional ingredient, the feeling factor, all encompassed in excitement. We are to consider, "Pure joy" when we encounter tough and trying times in our life

(James 1:2). God says that His joy lives inside each one of His children (John 15:11). You know there will be joy and laughter in heaven so why can't we bring a little piece of that fun down here to earth (Luke 15:7)?

So what is it that robs you of your joy? Why do you shy away from laughter with your colleagues? A good laugh can show realness and tear down walls of hierarchy. You don't need to quit your day job and become a Saturday night stand-up comedian to be able to laugh a little. Laughter is not some art or gift; it's a conscience choice. If you commute each day in traffic like I do, you see a lot of folks behind the wheel that could use a little laughter and a friendly smile. If you let nature take it course, it will choose the easy path and end up in anger. Too many people are too serious about life. Life is a zoo and it needs to be more of a carnival. It can be that if you assume your role as a fun person with a sense of humor looking at life and its curve balls with a smile and a chuckle. We as leaders need to be the pacesetters when it comes to having fun and living out Christ's joy in a dead world.

Begin this process by reading funny columns and comics in your newspaper. Go to the bookstore and spend some time in the humor section of the store with a cup of coffee. Start hanging around some joyful folks and see if some of that joy doesn't rub off. Play a non-demeaning practical joke on one of your friends. Do something today that is out of your comfort zone and far from normality. Look up clean jokes.com on the Internet at your lunch break and satisfy your masked desire with a good gut laugh. Go to a party dressed up like your living in the '70s wearing polyester. In other words live a little! You'll make life a better place and people will wonder what you've been drinkin.' You can tell them that you have Jesus joy, deep, deep, down in your heart. I don't think that Jesus died on a cross so that His followers would roam the planet with a frown smeared on their face. I think what John 10:10 ["I have come that you might have life and have it abundantly"] tells us to do is model the love of Christ through our outpouring of a joyful spirit.

8

Personal Disciplines

You see it a lot these days, in bookstores, on bumper stickers, and even worn by the late great PGA golfer Payne Stewart. It's those WWJD bracelets that are catalyst for reminding followers of Christ to ask in all circumstances they find themselves in, what would Jesus do? This is a great question to ask if you know your Bible. I was given one of those bracelets by my eldest son and wore it for a while until I started applying it. By this I mean, I found myself not really knowing what Jesus would do so I began an all out study of the gospels and specifically the parables, metaphors and symbolic stories Jesus told. One verse haunted me because I didn't quite know what to do with it. It was Luke 2:52 and it says, "And Jesus continued to grow: intellectually-wisdom; physically-stature; spiritually- favor with God; socially-favor with man."

Now, the word picture that was immediately painted on the canvas of my mind was a fine-tuned four-cylinder engine. It has four spark plugs and they have written on them: intellectual, physical, spiritual and social. I'm no mechanic but I do know that if one plug in your engine goes bad, your engine begins to knock and run improperly. You take it to a garage for repair and they will replace the bad plug to get you back out on the road again. What Dr. Luke is telling us here is [he does understand the function of the body], we need balance in our lives. Not only spiritually, that's only one plug, but in multiple areas. Now to achieve this goal, it takes understanding this is a, "process" not a destination. Leaders need to exemplify this process to those that follow. Remember, leaders are more responsible before God for their actions. God is looking for some F.A.T. people, Faithful-Available-Teachable. Do you qualify as a leader?

Intellectual and spiritual balances are two of the four plugs in your life [Luke 6:40]. I heard a quote once that read, "I'd rather drink from a running stream than a stagnant pool." Spiritual development is a part of a much larger picture; it can't be our only concern. Don't forget that leaders are readers and readers are leaders. Charles T. Jones said, "What you will be in five years will be determined by the people you associate with and the books you read." There are two factors of influence in peoples' lives, people you're around and the books you read [most importantly the Bible]. As a leader, you should enroll in continuing education to keep your mind sharp and in tune with what's going on around you. Not compartmentalized but integrated in all aspects of life. Do you spend daily time reading and meditating in and on the scriptures? Do you read books that give you tools for the journey we call leadership? Do you teach others that which you are learning?

The next plug in our engine that we need to look at is

the physical. Do you think that Jesus got daily exercise on his long walks as He ministered and lead the people in the ancient Near East? Do you think Jesus found time to eat healthy during his busy schedule? Do you think he got the proper rest needed to "fulfill His Fathers Will?" Are we as Christians prone to humanity? The answers are: yes; yes; yes; yes! There is as much hope for the body as your soul in your Bible, yet we live in the most obese society in the world. You may have your spiritual and intellectual plugs firing but your "temple" is falling apart. Guess what, you're out of balance and not fully productive. There are not many pastors, leaders, parents, and teachers broadcasting the message of staying physically fit. Let me say that exercise looks different to everyone yet you need to look to see if you're doing it. Exercise keeps your muscles firm and helps organs; particularly your heart and lungs, to work better. You may bike, run, play a sport, swim, walk, lift weights, do aerobics of some form but at least you doing something to show a lost culture that your God doesn't live in junk! (2 Cor.6:16) The guru of physical fitness and a friend of mine has a clinic in Dallas called the Cooper Aerobics Clinic. Dr. Ken Cooper told me that by exercising, proper rest and diet, that I could add anywhere from 5 to 15 years onto my ministry [not my life]. Taking your physical self seriously [not worshipping your body] can help me keep at my proper weight, give me more energy, handle stress better, keep my perspective on life positive and allow me to feel good about my physical self as I lead others.

Diet is so important because what you eat is what you

become. Good intake, good output. Did you ever wonder how the early church made it without coffee and doughnuts? I hear so many Christians argue over drinking beer and wine and if it's right or wrong, yet if fellow believers over eat, you don't hear anyone rebuke them for it. Remember, gluttony is a sin too (Prov. 23:20 and Matt. 11:19). What would happen if I walked into your church one Sunday morning falling down drunk? What if I were to walk in 50 pounds overweight? What's the difference? Why allow one extreme yet not the other? Eat what you need [not necessarily what you want] but don't stuff yourself. Make sure when you eat it's balanced nutrition with portions of fruit and vegetables, dairy, proteins, carbohydrates, and fats [taking vitamin and mineral supplements if needed].

Do you get enough sleep? Scientists still don't know exactly why but they do know that a person deprived of sleep would die within a few weeks. Sleep provides rest and helps you recover form fatigue on top of helping the brain to process and record things you have learned and experienced. Exercise is clinically linked to help you move into deep, sound, R.E.M [Rapid Eye Movement] sleep. Are you running on fuel or fumes by getting 4-6 hours sleep. The younger you are the more sleep you need. If you are not giving your body the rest and relaxation, exercise or nutrition it needs, then the physical plug causes your whole body to run poorly.

Socially is the final plug we need to check and see how it's firing. Do you know any lost people? Remember in Matthew 4:19 that God has not called us to be keepers of the aquarium but fishers of men and women? If you are in fulltime ministry work as a career, do you fellowship with any non-believers? As a balanced leader or minister of the gospel, you need input on leading from all types: little kids, teenagers, singles, and senior citizens from a variety of ethnic origins. Get to know those you lead whether it be employees, family members, teammates, students or whomever you lead. This is how you can answer questions they are asking instead of those they could care-less about. Can you carry on a conversation with those who differ with you in religious belief, color, socioeconomics, age, gender, and politics? As a leader, you CAN agree to disagree which could threaten your own belief and opinions but it may challenge them too.

Let me summarize, we all are in process here. We need to enjoy the journey God leads us on at His pace and encompassed in His plan. The truth of the matter is that a life that is paralyzed by "satisfaction" is decaying. How can I improve the areas I'm weak in? Begin by self-examination in the four areas we have been addressing and be honest with your answers. Ask your pastor, spouse, friends and children how balanced you are in process. The unexamined life is a dangerous place for any leader to put him or herself into. Experience doesn't make you better unless it's evaluated yet you can't take it as a personal threat. Get some goals that are clear and concise, direct and simple, significant and worthy, realistic and obtainable, measurable and timely, concrete and organized, biblical and ethical. Have a strategy to attain those goals, and accountability to maintain them. Ask for a touch from God to commit to sticking with your goals. Is it tough? Yes, but when the going gets tough, the followers of Christ should shine the brightest and step up to the plate as the example!

9

Your Calling

I was once on a two week mission trip to the island of Trinidad and Tobago in the Caribbean. I saw an old sign that has brain branded me ever since. It was a takeoff of the old proverb, "A chain is only as strong as its weakest link." This had an unfamiliar twist of that old cliché which read, "The brain is a strong as its weakest think." How many times do we have one of those, "Weak think" moments and make a wrong decision that not only affects us but those around us? Especially when it comes to what you do in this life.

Does God call those that follow Him down specific paths? Let us take a look in His word. Abraham was called to be the father of all nations. Moses and Joshua were called to lead God's people, Daniel to be obedient, Job to endure, Jonah to go to a hostile environment, Jesus to do the will of His father, Billy Graham and Dr. Bill Bright to be evangelists, Hudson Taylor to go to the mission field, George Mueller to minister to orphans, Corrie Ten Boom to write about concentration camps, James Dobson to be spokesman for the family. Yes, God does call His followers to take specific steps of faith for Him. Guess what, you don't retire from your calling! Your career is what you get paid for; your calling is what stems from your passions.

God's calling to His sheep first to conversion, which means I'm saved. Secondly, God calls his children to transformation, which means, I'm changing. And lastly, God is calling His followers to faithfulness, which means I'm committed at home; with my money, as a person of integrity; as a faithful mate; and as a parent. I once heard a great definition of faithfulness that was, "A long obedience in the same direction." Amen.

A "Calling" is what you do as you work out of your strengths column. So how do I zero in on my "Calling" and take aim on my unique potential as a leader? You must realize your God designed potential, kind of your spiritual DNA, which makes you different than anyone else on the planet, past, present and future (Ps. 139). You need to realize you have a unique: network of people; heritage; hardships; growing up environment; opportunities; resources, stories, alliances, mate, children, temperament. You have God honoring passions built inside you as standard equipment, a gift from heaven. So many leaders are living a passion-less life in our faith. Is it OK to do what God intended me to do? Adam and Eve got up every morning in the Garden of Eden and did whatever they wanted to do and it was "good" with God. You first must align your heart and passions with God's heart (1 Sam.13: 14). God's Kingdom purposes are to be apart of your passions so the whole world will know there is a God (1 Sam.17: 46). In Luke 19:10, God's purpose today is redemptive and to seek and save the lost. What is God up to and about? What does God view as success?

One phenomenon that I have noticed is how Christians get, "Pigeon holed" into doing what they do worst. This is when your passion fizzles and the joy is sucked right out of your life. Once you start working within your gifts you will notice others sarcastically cutting you down because they are jealous and envious of you because they have settled for second best. A quote that reminds me of this says, "The higher the monkey climbs in the tree, the more of his butt you can see." People love talking bad about leaders who are utilizing their God given gifts for the glory of the kingdom. This is where you as a leader need to gracefully not get "Eaten by the minnows." What I mean by this is being hypersensitive as a leader and taking every stab, cut or accusation to heart, which paralyzes your progress. As a leader, dealing with and leading others is always going to have this as an issue. Everyone is gunning for the top seeded team so why would it be any different in our social pecking order. As you receive criticism, analyze it and if it is true work towards changing. If it's laced with hidden agendas and impure motives, forget about it and move on (Col. 3:23). All I have to say about that [sounds like Forest Gump] is this. If you can't stand the smell of sheep, don't be a shepherd!

What is your gifting? What makes you unique from everyone else? I remember an opening scene in the children's movie Antz where this one certain ant is lying on a sofa receiving counseling from a psychiatrist about his significance. The shrinks' answer, "You are insignificant. You're one ant in a colony of one million." That is the sort of answer that would put anyone in a straightjacket. In Psalms 139:14 God's counsel is that we are all "Fearfully and wonderfully made" and not just another bar code number.

Do you know what your reasons are for being here on this planet? What is your purpose and calling in this vapor life in which we live with no guarantees of time? Trust me here; I'm not going to give you some self-help theology or A+B=C formula for success. It's not that simple. What I am going to do is point you back to the textbook and a powerful passage that mentor and teacher the apostle Paul gives to a younger Timothy (1 Timothy 4:14-16). "Do not neglect the spiritual gift within you. Go to great pains with these {gifts} things; be absorbed in them so that your progress may be evident to all. Pay close attention to yourself and your teaching; persevere in these things, for as you do this, you will insure salvation both for yourself and for those who hear [and see] you."

The wrong interpretation here is working for your salvation or a call to be a preacher. The correct faith lesson to apply here is that you, yes you, have God given gifts that are to be given back to your heavenly Father. Why? So that those that see your progress will not give you the credit but glorify God. In other words, people who size you up will realize you couldn't develop or train yourself to produce the product your producing so it must be from a divine touch. Zechariah 4:6 says, "Not by power, not by might but by Spirit says the Lord." It isn't about you and how you pull yourself up by your own bootstraps...one must ask, "Where did I get those boots anyway?" Remember, God doesn't call the qualified...He qualifies the called! Your phone is ringin.'

10

Empowerment

Leadership isn't what happens when you're there. It's what happens when you're not there. Effective delegation is the key to strong leadership because the very foundation of leadership is motivating others to personal and spiritual growth. Finding that untapped potential buried inside each individual. People tend to exceed expectations when they are lead by someone who cares about them and has their best interest in mind. One way of showing someone you care for them is for them to learn and take on new responsibilities. This is true in the market place, a church, team, as well as the home in child rearing.

Exodus 18:21-23 is a prime example of a Biblical way to empower others. I'll give you the condensed version but read it for yourself to get the full affect. Moses was leading a bunch of whinny-baby Israelites [about 3 million] and not only was he tapped out from the management side but the natives were fighting amongst themselves with no referee. Moses' father-in-law, Jethro, sees the troubled son-in-law at wits end and decides to offer a bit of relative advice. That advice in 21st Century interpretation, delegate you bonehead and spread some responsibility! The people became manageable and the problems became overcomeable.

Remember in the Disney movie *Dumbo*, there was a unique way that the big-eared elephant became an instant success in the traveling circus. Do you remember what that ingenious way was? This was done by a mouse by the name of Timothy that had a "magic feather" that stimulated Dumbo with his oversized ears to fly. What sort of magic feather do you have to get others to exceed their own capabilities and expectations? Empowering others to excellence both spiritually and occupationally is one of the greatest satisfactions a leader can feel. You as a leader can not do it all [even though I'm sure you've tried]. When you learn this fact, you will see your family, employees and staff have greater satisfaction and motivation.

So how do you do this? First you're going to have to have faith not only in those you're delegating to but faith in God (Heb. 11:1). When you delegate and give a person a specific job, be specific and clear about what you'd like to see accomplished. When the facts are clear, decisions are easy! Don't communicate poorly and expect the person your delegating to fill in the blanks. Don't expect too much too soon. Encourage their initial efforts and realize this is your opportunity to help others grow by doing and gaining experience. Don't micro-manage them to death but give them space to find their style for doing a task and room to make a few mistakes and learn from them. You might be pleasantly surprised at how creative people can be when they have the freedom to grow and learn. Clarify your expectations by telling them exactly what is expected of them from the get-go. Don't tell them there is no deadline or rush on the task when in your mind you think a "no rush" job should be done in a week or less. Time means different things to different people so there is no clear definition unless you as the leader define it for them.

Empowerment means when you ask a person to do a job, you give them the power and the resources to get the job done. So many leaders delegate an important task but have all sorts of strings and controls put on the person being delegated to as they walk away. Affirm the person you've just asked to do a job by telling others about your confidence in that person [magic feather theology]. Once you've delegated a job, find the right way to manage it. Seek a balanced approach that lies between micro-managing someone's every move and totally forgetting about the delegated responsibilities. This looks different to every leader. One way to do this is to set interim goals for the person. By setting goals, you can monitor progress at critical stages. You'll see if tough problems are on the horizon and you can detect them early and see if help is needed. Keep an open door policy so folks know you are accessible and approachable to talk to you about anything.

Social scientists have proven that behavior which is followed by something pleasant, like praise, tends to be reinforced and is more likely to be repeated. In the bestseller book: *The One Minute Manager,* it says to "catch people in the act of doing the right thing and tell them." To be effective though, it needs to be immediate, specific and genuine. At the end of the task there needs to be praise and celebration for a job well done [Jesus did this in John 1:47]. If something goes wrong, don't heap blame on the person who might have made a mistake. Self examine and see if a portion of the blame should return to you, the leader, for not delegating the task more effectively.

Lastly, delegating is an art and it frees you from many time consuming activities. It will allow you the time to handle what's most important to conduct your students, players, employees, church staff or family. It really frees you to do what you do best while at the same time allowing others to grow. E. Stanley Jones writes in his book *A Song of Ascent,* "I hold a crown a few inches above my people's heads and watch them grow into it." Delegating is what makes your job more fun and enjoyable. Watch others grow in confidence as they develop new skills. This also is the foundation for ministry and what Jesus did best, empowering others! A final word of caution, Jesus realized that there were some things He absolutely could not delegate [discipling the disciples, suffering persecution, dying on the cross]. Some leaders go crazy on the delegation stuff and end up becoming very lazy. Those that answer to you and follow you need to see your production towards common goals as well as you need to see theirs. A true leader gets excited about facilitating someone else's success.

11

Success

One of the greatest formula's for success comes right from God in Joshua 1:19. Here lies the keys to success as communicated thousands of years ago to a young man named Joshua. Joshua was born in Egypt, served on Pharaoh's army as a personal attendant to Moses during the year at Mount Sinai. He was commissioned by God before Moses death to be his successor and lead them on a conquest of Canaan. This story takes place during the spring at the famous bank of the Jordan River while the usually slow running stream was now swollen to flood stage. Moses, who was Joshua's mentor, has just died after leading the people of Israel from slavery and performing miraculous feats. They were headed to the "Land of milk and honey" better known as the Promise Land where the brutal Canaanites. The only obstacle was getting millions of doubting Jews across this river. Now Joshua is going to get a message from God on the how-to's of achieving success.

The first thing you read in verse 2 is where God tells Joshua to "get ready." As a leader you need to constantly be getting prepared for God's daily callings. God calls each of us to purity, faithfulness and thankfulness. In that same verse, God tells Joshua to "go" and cross the river with all those people. I think we need to mention it says you and "all these people" need to enter the land that God had given to them. We as leaders have a tendency to do things alone. Most leaders are very talented and self motivated so they would just as soon go do it alone for the sake of time. Little do they realize the dangers that await a "loner." I think of the Caribou in Alaska that stray from the heard. They are the ones the wolves pull down for supper. Those who ride alone usually fall flat on their face at some point in the journey.

Then God tells Joshua as you go, be "strong and courageous" in verse 6. We need to glean the hard fact that as a leader, there are no free rides and that leadership is going to cost you, not only in labor but also in people. The late great British Ruler, Winston Churchill summed it up best after a huge military victory speech to the British people saying, "Never, never, never, quit." Simply put and profoundly truthful. As a leader of thousands or a few, we need to realize adversity is a testing and purifying element of the process. As you go, you need to be strong in your faith and convictions and courageous because your strength will be challenged both physically and emotionally. In verse 7, we see another nugget, which tells us to "be careful to obey all the law." In other words leadership has a direct order of obedience to the divine precepts and truths of scripture. The greatest textbook on how to lead is found in the infallible Word of God. Notice it says to do "all" the law, not just what we like or what's easiest to obey. People have a strong tendency to do only what we like to do, not what we need to do. As a leader you need to be a cut above this sort of rationalization. Throughout this book, I'll remind you, the reader leader, that we all are guilty because of our sinfulness before God yet as a leader, you ARE more responsible to God (James 3:1). God is either going to bless you because you obeyed or judge you because you didn't. I realize that sort of statement doesn't preach well in our churches but it's truth derived from the Bible. In that same verse, Joshua is warned "do not turn from it to the right or the left." Let me give you a metaphor on this point. Remember when you were first learning to ride a bike without the training wheels? Or maybe you were teaching one of your children to ride a bike for the first time? Remember telling or being told not to look anywhere but straight ahead or you were going to do a face plant with road rash results? The devil will offer you something good to rob from you something great (James 1:17). As a leader you must stay focused on the task ahead, not on the past failures or side notes. Focus is what leaders need to do and do it well. Especially in the midst of the chaos and in the heat of the moment. Looking to the right or left is nothing more than a distraction that gets you off course.

Finally, we need to mediate on God's word day and night (verse 8). The word in the Hebrew for meditates means to regurgitate. Like a cow that has four stomachs and chews on its cud for nutritional value, we need to be "belching up" God's truths all the time, chewing on it a little bit throughout the day to gain spiritual nutrition for our tasks at hand and upcoming. Hopefully you spend time daily in Bible reading and study [if you don't, you should]. You should digest the wisdom you learn not just in the morning but also throughout the day. This is a key ingredient to effective Godly leadership.

So what? If I follow this formula for success, what are the results? Lets just take a look-see. The Lord says he will never leave you or forsake you in verses 5 and 9. If you ever feel like God has left you, ask yourself who left whom. God is not a quitter; he has staying power through the mountaintop and valley experiences of life. Another promise is that you will conquer and win in verse 3. This might and might not mean victory by the world's definition but it does by God's and that's all that matters. Lastly, you will be successful and prosper in verse 8. The definition here for success is that you will have success in being the leader God desires you to be. If you look at the whole book of Joshua you see success intermingled throughout the life of this leader. Yes, he does have his challenges but the final score reads victor!

12

Re-solving Conflict

I was at a cemetery once just reading the headstones of folks who had died, the dates they lived, and the words that relatives had inscribed in granite to describe this person's life here on earth. This one inscription caught my attention because this dear gentlemen's wife obviously wrote it and it read like this, "Here lies my dear husband Elmer, and may he rest in peace until we meet again." Now I'm no psychologist but if I was to psycho-analyze this couple's many years of marriage together, I can assume it had numerous fires that were put out by conflict resolution.

The older I get, the more I see why the Book of Romance [the best marriage and sex book in the Bible] the Song of Solomon, is only eight chapters total and it takes you from dating, to courting, to the marriage ceremony, to the honeymoon, through the late years of marital faithfulness. I see now why two out of eight chapters are dedicated to conflict. Why do you think this is? Maybe because you'll spend about 25 percent of your married life re-solving differences of opinion, styles, temperaments and perspectives with your spouse.

Conflict is everywhere and you best not deny it; you should best learn how to handle it constructively. Most have the attitude when conflict arises with your spouse, employee, fellow worker, kids or a friend that a win-lose attitude supercedes that of a win-win format. Just think, you can walk away content in a heated disagreement that difference of opinion is okay.

Ephesians 4:26 says, "Be angry yet do not sin; don't let the sun go down on your anger." There are two types of anger: sinful and righteous. Why do we show anger? Because our rights have been violated, we have been hurt or our expectations haven't been meet. For some people, it's safer to show anger than it is to acknowledge hurt. Anger is a very powerful weapon that if uncontrolled, can kill a relationship. Uncontrolled worldly anger can produce bitterness, cause depression and ultimately affect your relationship with God. Jesus exemplified "righteous" anger when he stormed the temple of the Lord and threw over slate tables and ran out all the tax collectors who had set up shop in God's holy house to conduct their business (Matt. 21:12-13). This gold nugget of scripture is (Eph.4:26) there because God knows in all of us dwells some type of anger. It is what we do with that anger that matters and how we conduct ourselves when experiencing anger. I heard a quote one time that said, "The tongue is the only tool that the more we use it, the sharper it gets." James 3:5-8 uses the metaphor to describe the tongue as a spark that starts a forest fire or a bit in a horse's mouth. In Genesis you see the, "You shall surely die" phrase that was told to Adam and Eve if they ate the forbidden fruit. This promise by God was played out in their two sons Cain and Abel as Cain killed Abel in cold blood in a field while his brother was working. So the first death in the Bible was a brutal act of murder.

When it comes to resolving conflict with anyone, you must first have the ground rules in place so all parties fight fair and play within the boundaries. What follows is a suggestion for those boundaries.

Acknowledge your personal contribution to the problem and agree on the way you will discuss resolving conflict.

Check your agenda's, motivation, and attitude.

Stick with the issue(s) at hand. Don't use past situations as "ammo." Speak truth but in love.

Eliminate from the conversation phrases like: "You always" or "You never."

Don't deal with issues that surround the problem. Identify the real issue(s).

Express yourself and your feelings with statements that begin with "I" instead of "You." [I is you focused; you is an attack]

Avoid analyzing the other person's character or behavior.

Accept criticism maturely and graciously. Avoid a counter attack. See if you're as willing to accept confrontation as you are to give it.

Avoid mind reading every word the person says or means by a particular comment.

Keep short accounts and don't let the sun go down on your anger [deal with it in a timely manner].

Don't attempt to win an argument. Seek mutual satisfying solutions to your disagreements.

No "Hitting below the belt" with cut-downs, character attacks or demeaning insults.

When a violation occurs in one of the above rules, call it, corral your emotions and start over if possible.

Note: Pick a neutral location and if necessary, get an outside, neutral, mediator to monitor this situation.

As a leader, you are constantly dealing with a variety of temperaments and personalities that bring into this life a complex web of baggage. The Apostle Paul and John Mark had conflict on a mission trip Jesus sent them on and it took time to reconciliate the relationships back to the way they were prior to the mishap. Winston Churchill once said, "Wars were not won by evacuations." You have to deal with the issue if you want to solve it. Be willing to forgive, not forget. God has not asked you to forget the reasons for the conflict or the pain inflicted [only He can do that] but He has asked you to choose to grant forgiveness with a good attitude. Forgiveness begins the process in which trust can be rebuilt. Chuck Swindoll said, "You have to blast before you can build." Luke 11:17 says, "A house divided will fall." You can't, NOT live in this unfair, fallen, sinful world without dealing with conflict. You're not going to have a garden with no weeds until you get to heaven so start pickin.' I realize in this mixed up world it looks more spiritual stuffing or suppressing your anger but that ain't God's way. Worldly anger is you focused and Godly anger is spirit controlled. Don't react to the person or situation that has rubbed you the wrong way. Respond the way God would have you respond, righteously! Yes, it is possible and probable.

13

Stamina

The mad dash we call life doesn't go to the swift or the strong but to the one that endures. This race is not a sprint where the start is so key, but a marathon, where staying power matters. I heard an interview on CBS Sports with David Duval prior to the PGA Masters golf tournament and he said a very profound statement, "Today's preparation is tomorrow's performance." I saw an ancient Japanese Proverb on a cup of yogurt that I was eating that said, "Fall seven times, stand up eight."

The effective leader is aware of the importance of stamina. They know the importance of the energy it takes in the role of leadership and consciously tries to build up his or her own energy level. You can do this by exercise, rest and learning your limits. My dad who raises and trains Quarter and Thoroughbred race horses uses a term when a fast horse, "Runs through his bit." This means that the jockey on top of this mass of muscle needs to pace the horse for 8 furlongs to complete the race successfully and excel at the finish line. This "running through your bit" happens to leaders who don't realize they need to conserve energy as well as use it at the proper times.

My good friend, Bo Mitchell, once told me that the secret to success is simply to last. This involves the principle of stamina-staying power. Recognize that some difficulties and problems can be overcome, not necessarily eliminated, by stamina. God will honor tenacity and your faith. Read (Matthew 10:22; 1 Cor. 9:12; 2 Tim 2:12).

There is little doubt in my mind that the demands of being a leader are huge and no matter how well you prepare and plan, the journey is difficult. You have to endure disappointment (Rom. 5:3), have resilience about you to bounce back and make a setback be a comeback. One of the duties of leadership is to present a positive outlook about the future and to articulate the direction and steps that need to be taken to overcome a challenge that has been laid before you. The schedule of a leader is difficult in that there are definite times when the pressures and demands WILL be onerous.

I want you to do something for me and think of your schedule and week as 21 separate increments. By that I mean you have seven mornings, seven afternoons, and seven evenings. If you're going to be an effective Godly leader you should NOT be working more than fourteen of these increments or you are "running through your bit" and likely not going to finish the race. There is a challenging poem I want you to read that is titled: "Two Kinds of People" by Ella Wheeler Wilcox.

> There are two kinds of people on earth today,
> Just two kinds of people no more I say,
> Not the good or the bad, for tis' well understood,

The good are half bad and the bad are half good.

Not the happy and sad, for the swift flying years

Bring each man his laughter and each man his tears.

Not the rich or the poor, for to count a man's wealth

You must first know the state of his conscience and health.

Not the humble and proud, for in life's busy span

Who puts on vain airs is not counted a man.

NO! The two kinds of people on earth I mean

Are the people who lift and the people who lean!

Wherever you go you will find the world's masses

Are ever divided in just these two classes.

And, strangely enough, you will find, too, I wean,

There is only one lifter for twenty who lean.

This one question I ask. Are you easing the load

Of overtaxed lifters who toil down the road?

Or are you a leaner who lets others bear

Your portions of worry, labor, and care?

As a lifter you apply the sabbatical principle, even though you may not be working for a church, on a daily, weekly and monthly basis. Make it a point to take off some minute's every day to get out of the "fire" and pressures of your duties and responsibilities. Take some slots of time away each week and month to recharge. Get some time of "solitude" [This is discussed in a separate chapter in this book]. Don't deprive yourself or family of vacations and holiday breaks. Why? Because this principle will help to keep the tank full and energy level high, which is, needed to "finish strong." This time will help you to be more sharp and productive for the Glory of the Lord (Luke 21:19). Strength and endurance are needed commodities of an effective leader but can't be obtained unless they are recognized and prioritized.

14

Art of Communication

Did you know that affirming others through the art of communication could be the greatest ministry you ever do in your life? 1 Corinthians 4 deals with the gifts God has given each of us and the gift of "exhortation" happens to be one of them. General U.S. Grant retained an incompetent officer on his staff for one reason and one reason only, "If he can understand my orders….. anyone can." Proverbs 24:3 states, "by wisdom a house is built, and by understanding is established." Many people want nothing more than someone to care enough to listen to them and value their opinion. Communicating is no piece of cake. There was a company in Chicago that went bankrupt only one year after making a multi-million dollar profit. Why? They failed to understand what business they were in. They thought they were in the bobby-pin business instead of the hair-care business. When women stopped using bobby pins, the company sank. As a leader you need to know what business you are in and that includes the communication business. John Milton Gregory says "It is the teacher's mission…by sympathy, by example, and by every means of influence-by objects for the senses, by facts for intelligence- to excite the mind of pupils, to stimulate their thoughts... The greatest of teachers said: "The seed is the word." The true teacher stirs the ground and sows the seed." The key to communication is seeking to understand <u>then</u> be understood.

What does it take for genuine communication to occur? Three things: Time; trust, and transparency. All communication has three components: intellect, emotion and volition. This is something I know, something I feel, and something I'm doing. Understanding someone else's perspective will increase levels of communication. Most co-workers, teammates, marriages, and friendships never deepen their relationship because they talk at a comfortable, surface level. Take for instance, the "cliché" level, which is not sharing much at all. Then you'll migrate to the "fact" level, which is sharing facts that you know to be true like the weather outside. Next comes the "opinion" level, which is sharing what you think, or your personal opinion on a certain matter. Then comes the "emotional" level and that's where you share how you feel [this term is foreign to a lot of men] about a certain situation or circumstance. The deepest level you can go to is the level of "transparency" and that is where you share with someone who you are. As you move from the cliché down the communication graph to transparency, you will see the degree of trust, commitment, and friendship deepen.

The word communication comes from the Latin word **communis**, which means to find commonality that encourages communication. The greater the commonality, the greater the potential for real communication to occur. When people are born they bring into this world varying patterns and ways of communicating. Each one of my three sons communicated their first words in such an array of ways. They are no different than you and the way you try to convey a message to someone. When I was in junior high I remember a series of letters that stood for something unique: NBNWJD. This means: No better, no worse, just different. Just because you and a fellow employee, spouse, teammate, or acquaintance have different communication styles, they both can be effective if done properly. People need to extend each other grace and allow freedom for differences in styles for expressiveness. Some people are cognitive communicators and others emotional. One is more closed and has difficulty expressing their feelings and others have difficulty confining their emotions. Childhood programming and environments come into play when a person does or does not communicate properly. This programming establishes a pattern in a person's life of suppression and repression of emotions. Today's media stereotypes men to be non-emotion and not transparent because it shows weakness. NFL coach Dan Reeves was quoted as saying to his players at pre-game pep talk, "men, never, never, let them see you sweat." Have you ever seen the old western movie hero John Wayne change a baby's diaper? A poor self-worth and image can cause someone to fear rejection so they keep their conversations at a cliché level. Pride comes into play in a lot of men's lives because they think that sharing how they feel and who they are takes away their "manliness." Even a false sense of spirituality makes us hesitant to share ourselves with anyone.

In the fine art of communication, expressing yourself is going to involve risk. If I was to ask your spouse or best friend if you are "emotionally intimate" with them what would they say? Adam and Eve were "both naked and not ashamed" (Gen. 2:25). Being naked with someone, and I don't mean physically, involves the disclosure of your thoughts, feelings and needs. No matter who you are or what type of life you've lived previously, you must have all three of these key ingredients to communicate effectively.

Let me land this plane and give you some practical steps to becoming a better communicator. Proverbs 13:15 says, "good understanding produces favor, but the way of the treacherous is hard." Are you a person of understanding or are you treacherous? Do you seek to understand before being understood? Ask questions that can't be answered with a yes or no answer. Clarify what you're saying and be specific with your intent. Be sensitive to other people's values and opinions. They may be telling you something about themselves in their stance. The management expert, Peter Drucker once said, "The most important thing in communication is to hear what isn't being said."

I'll close with a cute story I read about a 3 year old boy who was with his father one sunny Saturday afternoon, running errands around town. The boy was eating an apple in the backseat of the family mini-van and asked his father a simple question, "Dad, why is my apple turning brown?" "Because," the father explained, "after you ate the skin off, son, the meat of the apple came into contact with the air which caused it to oxidize thus changing the molecular structure and turning it into a different color." There was a long silence then the boy asked softly, "Daddy, are you talking to me?" The art of **communis** is a lifelong process and takes work yet it's well worth the effort.

15

Art of Listening

If you've ever taken a human anatomy class you probably never noticed this basic observation. God custom designed the head with two ears and one mouth. I find it ironic that you can open and close your mouth but not your ears. Did you know that you listen 5x faster that you speak? Did you know that you couldn't learn a thing while your talking? Good listeners manifest an attitude that encourages communication. James 1:19 "Let everyone be quick to hear, slow to speak and slow to anger."

A few years back in the Chicago newspaper, an anonymous reader placed a brilliant classified that read, "Will listen for 5 minutes for $5.00." After his first week of running the classified, he had over 200 callers and made around $1000.00! What does that tell you about our culture and its needs? Listening to someone transmits a very strong signal of care and value to a person. Have you ever been telling someone something that is very important to you and they are looking over your shoulder at something or someone else in the room that they value more than your story?

A poor listener will manifest habits that stifle a conversation and relationship and stirs up misunderstanding. Pseudo listening means to act like you're interested but you're faking interest. A selective listener will tune in only when there are points of interest. A protective listener does not hear anything that might be threatening to them or their self-image. Listen with an attitude that the person's comments you are listening to are priority and have a willingness and attitude of acceptance to understand what they are trying to communicate. Listen with an attitude of desire clarification. Ask specific questions and paraphrase in order to get at the meaning of what's being communicated like, "What did you mean when you said _____?" or "Of all that you just said, what do you most want me to understand?" A good listener will work on proper habits that will enhance communication with others such as eye contact, and body language. When Lyndon B. Johnson was a junior senator from Texas he kept a sign on his office wall that read, "You ain't learnin' nothin' when you're doin' all the talkin.'" Let others confide in you as a leader because it may not help you, but it surely will help them.

Most people tend to speak about 180 words a minute, but they can listen at 300 to 500 words a minute. Paul Tillich a German theologian and philosopher once wrote, "The first duty of love is to listen." Author Dale Carnegie says, "You can make more friends in two weeks by becoming a good listener than you can in two years trying to get other people interested in you." Plutarch of Ancient Greece: "Know how to listen, and you will profit even from those who talk badly." Woodrow Wilson, the twenty-eighth American president, once said, "The ear of the leader must ring with the voices of the people." Here are a few helpful suggestions for listening:

- Look the person you're talking with in the eyes.

- After hearing their name, say it five times in your head.

- Ask good questions about the person.

- Start the conversation out on a personal note, not a business one.

- End the conversation with their name, "_____ it has been a pleasure visiting with you."

- Don't become distracted and lose eye contact during the conversation.

- Always be respectful, polite, and courteous.

Listening is the key to learning and leading. As a leader, to be effective you must begin to discipline yourself to listen first then speak. Very few leaders take the fine art of listening seriously. They often feel that they are a storeroom of knowledge that needs to be emptied. Most leaders think a person is looking to them for solutions when often, all they want is empathy and a listening ear. There is a time to do both, listen and speak, and the key is knowing the timing of both. Try active, focused, listening the next time you're in a conversation and see what results you will attain. I think you'll be surprised at the end result.

16

Casting Vision

Leaders don't delegate establishing vision and direction. A leader is the primary source of direction and vision. The question there in lies, how well do you cast vision? Do those you lead trust you enough to follow your vision? Every great mission begins with a vision from the Lord as you seek divine direction. A vision is not a distorted dream at night while you're asleep. It's not something seen in a trance or ecstasy. It is a supernatural leading by the Spirit of God that conveys a revelation. It is an unusual discernment or foresight into the future. A true visionary is one whose ideas or projects are impractical to many but not too big for God. Visionary's dream of God-size feats working through the faithful and obedient. Visionary's dream impossible dreams. Leaders dream big and small dreams. Because we dream, we build our hopes, we make plans. We believe we will succeed with God's hand. The dreams become very real to us. And yet, one off day can change the picture dramatically. The vision can be shattered. As strong as they are, dreams can be rather fragile and fleeting. It can be devastating and disappointing and difficult to handle when a vision is shattered.

Because of this headache some choose not to have dreams. Many will get down on themselves for ever having and sharing a vision in the first place. Many leaders will conclude that they are failures because the vision was shattered. Through this disappointment, which is very real, the fact remains that in the vast majority of cases, a leader is much better off for sharing the vision. It is because of dreaming, a leader is more productive, reaches higher, accomplishes more, and is ultimately happier. Vision casting usually represents a challenge or an opportunity to achieve. Vision usually causes us to act in a positive way to fulfill the dream. Where would we be without vision? Scripture tells us that, "Where there is no vision, the people perish"(Prov. 29:18). Without vision for the future of a company, ministry or family, we would accomplish little. At times, we limit ourselves and begin to accept life as it is and fall into a false sense of security and comfort, never daring to step out in faith. Change is usually for the better and is what makes life interesting. Vision is what causes us to grow and set goals for ourselves. Vision casting is what allows us to live life to its fullest (Eph. 3:20).

In order to accomplish or achieve anything in this life, we must be able to picture in our minds the desired result. Leader's must have a *vision* for where they are going, surround themselves with *leadership* to pull off the vision, then develop a *system* in which to function. This is the responsibility of the vision caster to paint a clear picture on the canvas of human minds. They must have a strategy for fulfilling the vision and commitment on the part of those who buy into the dream and the deal. Vision fulfillment requires action! Without action, it's nothing more than a fleeting thought. Focus on the result and implement the vision. The more obsessed and passionate we are with the vision the more likely it will happen. When we have a vision or idea go sour, we need to reload and dare to dream again. It's important we not let a setback make us bitter or disillusioned. Since the vision was in the mind originally, we need to replace shattered dreams with new ones when God initiates them. As a leader, your visions are the very future of a home, church, team, company, etc., that will determine your way of life. Shattered dreams are necessary sometimes to cause us to dream even bigger dreams the next time. Don't be afraid of change or stepping out of your comfort zone. Jesus said in Matthew 9:17 "Don't pour new wine in old wine skins." This means that old ways of thinking or doing things sometimes aren't the best. Christ himself was the master vision caster as he told His audiences about a special place called heaven. Be an, "Out of the box" thinker and see where it takes you!

17

Imagination

There is a term that has been flying around corporate conference rooms for years. The term is, "Thinking outside the box" and it means to think beyond the obvious. Walt Disney was a prime example of this as he purchased flooded, worthless swamp land in central Florida years ago and envisioned a Mecca conglomeration of theme parks for kids and families. Why? Because he knew to plan for the future he would need thousands of acres in real estate to do this and he didn't want his fortune to be eaten up in land costs, so he thought outside the box. On that useless property today, sits: The Magic Kingdom, Epcot, Animal Kingdom, MGM Studio's, several water parks, five star resorts, and an intricate network of transportation systems. Today, the property is the No. 1 tourist destination in the world.

When the Disney Corporation was about to break ground on The Magic Kingdom, Walt Disney decided to have a huge cookout on the site and invited every worker and sub-contractor to attend this huge one-day event. There were bulldozer operators, concrete layers, drywall specialists, ride engineers, architects, electricians, air conditioning installers, welders, roofers, carpenters, telephone technicians, computer programmers and many more. Walt had the engineers and architects design a detailed mini model of The Magic Kingdom, equipped with the castle, lakes, sculptured hedges, theaters, food stands and fun rides like Space Mountain. Why did he go to the trouble and expense to feed thousands of workers and show them this model? Because he wanted every worker to see more than concrete, nails, metal or blueprints. He wanted them to be a part of the deal and the dream. Talk about creative and imaginative, can you believe thousands of people bought into a wonderland in a wasteland? Why? Because then the laborers would not only invest their talent and trade but their hearts in what they were doing. Proverbs 29:18 says this, "Where there is no vision, the people perish." God knows the importance of casting a vision to the people. Scripture describes people as "sheep" and there is a reason for that. We all need a Shepherd. We need protection and direction as we move from pasture to pasture, phase of life to phase of life.

If you go to Disney's Epcot Park, you can experience a ride called, "Imagination Station." I loved to go on this ride because the whole theme is to encourage its attendees to, "think outside the box" in whatever arena they exist. To encourage you not to ride down the path of normality but to blaze the trail of creativity. Creativity is not some special gift or anointing from God, but a mindset that few choose to encounter. Maybe you are the organized planned type personality that struggles with out-of-the-box thinking. What should you do? Surround yourself with people who will challenge you and the creativity within you. All of us have a specific bent of creativity and all you need is someone to jar you out of the rut in which you make decisions. Families, businesses, teams, churches, groups need to extend themselves to cutting edge thinking. If you don't have someone who will step out and try something new, then hire someone who will or make it a conscience choice to change your normal, routine ways. The world is a better place because of creative people like Thomas Edison, Jonas Saulk, Bill Walsh, Elisa Morgan, Michael Dell and Bill Bright.

In 1968, he was born into poverty in a foreign land. Sammy Sosa learned baseball with a milk carton for a glove and a stick for a bat. In 1998, he along with Big Mac made the game of Major League Baseball fun again by shattering the home run record, and captured America's heart because they chose to be thinking outside the norm. How about you?

18

Integrity

You hear it a lot these days after the Promise Keepers movement. The word is integrity and the Hebrew word for it indicates something solid, of substance. A person of integrity is indeed a complete, mature and whole being. Vernon Grounds of Denver Seminary defines integrity "The antithesis of hypocrisy, sound all the way through, like a gold coin without alloy." The true leader merits the trust and respect of others because of his or her integrity, which takes precedence over any desire or gain. On his scale of values, spiritual values are seated No. 1. Moral and ethical values are next with social and human values, and then comes material values. Art Linkletter asked a little boy what his daddy did for a job. The boy took the microphone and said, "He is a policeman. He cuffs em', makes them spread eagle and throws folks in jail." Art then says, "Your mother must worry about him a lot" the boy quickly answers, "Nope, not really. She gets a lot of watches, jewelry, and other things out of the deal."

Integrity includes promise keeping. A promise is a commitment for the future whether it is a marriage vow, returning a phone call promptly, being on time to a meeting, or simply , "Letting your yes be yes and your no be no." (Matt. 5:37) A promise says, "To the best of my ability and if circumstances beyond my control don't stop me, I will do what I said I would do." No higher level of communication can be given to someone than to say "They keep their promises" [dependability]. There are two types of integrity tests; the test of adversity (Prov.24:10) and the test of prosperity. The test of adversity is when money fails, the audience doesn't respond, and you feel like you're in a wind tunnel losing your footing. The test of prosperity complicates life a bit when small things now become big. You now become the star of the show and you start reading your own press clippings and asking yourself for an autograph. Integrity is what and whom you are when no one is watching. Real integrity stays in place whether you encounter adversity or prosperity.

Personal integrity implies a firm stick-to-it mentality to a system of ethics. The wholeness of integrity demands a constant set of unbreakable values, not the use of one set in the workplace, another at home, and another at church. We need leaders to remember that integrity does not lie in what one says but in the way one lives. The leader sets the moral and spiritual overtones of an organization, family, team or church. A leader can't afford to wink at any breech of ethics, no matter how small or rewarding the opportunity may appear. Like Caesar's wife, the leader must be beyond any suspicion.

Winston Churchill said it best, "Technology is going faster that our morality." Does one person swimming up the social stream make a difference? In other words, does my integrity matter? To God most definitely, but remember, not to decide is to decide. It only took one vote to give Hitler the power to kill millions of prisoners. One vote brought Texas into the Union. Yes, you and your example do matter in our dark and tasteless society (Matt. 5:13-16).

Ask yourself an important question- what will you sell out for? How much is your integrity worth to you? As a leader these are questions you can't evade. We all need to daily refocus back to the cause and effect graph. We all need to draw another line in the sand [ultimatum] and keep the standard high. Integrity is not some special gift from God; it's a choice we, as leaders, have to make. As you get old and gray, you will look back on your choices and see that you make your decisions in this life then your decisions make you. A lasting legacy is the glue that holds it all together and it's laced with integrity and honesty. If it isn't, you'll leave nothing behind but a bunch of stink. Be a leader of integrity so that the world may know.

19

Handling Stress

The higher a man climbs in his field the greater will be his problems and stress. Stress is a constraining force or influence on a person. I was playing a game recently with a group of friends and we had the guy verses girl thing working. As you might expect, the girls were winning so I resorted to checking out the rules to see if they were cheating. The game was called Guesstures. It is a game of split-second charades with little use of gray matter and long on the quick and clever. I looked up a ruling that the girls claimed was illegal and read rule No. 1, "This game is not fair."

As a leader, you realize early in your calling that the game of life isn't fair either. There are constant clouds of anxiety and uncertainty hanging over your head. This lack of control causes stress with a capitol "S." You try to avoid it like a suppertime sales call but it knocks at your door. The issue is not to avoid it but to learn how to deal with it. Dealing with stress takes all shapes and forms for people. Some run from it, some deny it exists, some get angry, some quit, some get depressed and even some go as far as to try to cover it with drugs or alcohol.

Stress comes at you from every side and plays no favorites (2 Cor. 4:8). Stress is a man made element brought on by sin, not created by God. James 1:17 says, "Every good thing bestowed and every perfect gift comes down from the Father of lights in whom there is no variation or shifting shadows." In Genesis 3:8, you see that sin causes a constraining force or influence on Adam and Eve after they disobeyed God and ate the forbidden fruit. How did they handle it? They ran and hid from the Lord.

Stress is created from a plethora of spheres in life: marriage, rearing kids, job pressure, peer pressure, money and debt, unresolved conflict, health issues, death, unsafe environments, performance, trials, pressing needs, persecution from beliefs, hurtful words, and overbooked schedules. There is not a character in the scriptures that escaped the deadly grip of stress. Jesus cried out on the cross, "Father, if it be your will, remove this cup from me" (Luke 22:42). His disciples felt fear as a result of the stress (Matt. 17:6-7) yet Jesus came to them and said, "Arise, don't be afraid." Christ's desire is for His sheep to be fearless and graze a stress free pasture (Psalms 23).

Stress raises to the surface emotions like: fear, worry, discomfort, anger, and sadness. Fear can affect your physical well-being too. It can produce sleepless nights, nervous habits, degenerative heart conditions, and loss of weight from a lack of appetite. Of the entire negative side we dwell on when we think of stress, there is a positive side. Stress can be a masterful motivator for good if handled correctly. Stress can be the catalyst for giant leaps of personal as well as spiritual growth. It all depends on what you do with what you're dealt. Psalm 55:22 says to, "Cast your burdens upon the Lord." Why? Because the weary people produced by the stresses of life are called to come to the Lord, "Because His burden is easy and His yoke is light" and He will give you needed relief (Matt. 11:28). Taking your stress to a God who understands stress yet is not affected by it, is a sure fire way to see results. The prophet Isaiah says if you wait on the Lord, you will walk along life's journey and not grow weary of stressful situations (40:31).

I recall Peter and the walking on the water incident. Here is a professional fisherman out on the water looking at what appears to be a ghost. Jesus says to his men in the boat, "It is I." Peter, in typical fashion, says, "Lord, if it's you, bid me come." Jesus says come on. Letting go of the boats railing was probably one of the toughest things Peter ever did yet he did it. One of the disciples I'm sure reminded Peter in route that the waves are high and Peter realizes the fact and freezes, looks down, and begins to sink in the sea. He then says a great prayer, "Lord, save me." You can't eliminate a word from this prayer without changing the meaning. If this had been one of those long church prayers, Peter would have been twenty feet under the waters surface by the time it was over. Simplicity is all God needs from the helpless in time of need. When stress arises, give up to God a simple prayer and He'll answer the call with urgency. Now God may not rescue immediately but he is there for you and hears your cry. God may be teaching you something in the process but He won't let you drown in life's circumstances. All He is waiting on is for you to let go and walk to the foot of the cross in faith for deliverance. It's a scary walk but the

Savior is there to help.

So many Americans are all stressed up with no place to go. There is a place to go and that is the comfort of an understanding God. This is known as stress management. He will and wants to bare the burden of that cross called stress. Christ, the only atonement, has paid the price for stress on the cross so you and I, can live a stress-free life.

20

Synergy

The year I was a captain for the basketball team at Highland Park H.S. in Dallas, TX. We captains had a decision to make as the leaders of that team and that was to decide on a "theme" for the season. We came up with some catchy phrases but finally decided on, "There is no I in the word team."

The word synergy comes from the Greek, which means: working together. Webster's dictionary defines synergy to mean: interaction of discrete agencies such that the total effect is greater than the sum of the individual effects. In other words there is power in the pack! Each year in the great patriot state of New England there is a state fair. One of the attractions that bring contestants from all across the country is the draft horse-pulling contest. Farmers bring to the fair their prize brut animal to show-off its strength in pulling. Draft horses do more than pull beer wagons; they pull logs for loggers, plows for farmers and sleds for mountaineers. The contest is to match mass against muscle as the horse is hitched up to a wooden sled loaded with 55 gallon barrels filled with sand. The object is to see which horse can pull the most weight over a predetermined distance without stopping. The winner of the contest pulled 4640 pounds. While second place was close behind pulling 4280 pounds. At the medal ceremony following the contest, the 1st and 2nd place horse owners decided to hitch their draft horses together to see what they both would pull as a team. The results were astonishing; they pulled 12, 260 pounds. If you passed simple addition and subtraction class in school, you will see that both horses pulled individually a total of 8920 pounds. Hitched together they pulled another 3340 lbs. more! What a difference in performance is made when coupled with a partner.

There is a new phrase in our cyberspace world called, "Cocooning." Social forecasters describe the trends we as a nation are headed for and introduced this term. This term insinuates we as a people are crawling back into our own little worlds, alienating and isolating ourselves more and more. How often do you speak with voice mail rather than a real live person? How often do you communicate and do your shopping via Internet? Why? We are encouraged today to keep our distance and remain in our comfort zones because it safe there and little risk of being emotionally or physically hurt by our sinful, hateful, violent society. I often wonder how would Jesus have preached to the masses the Sermon on the Mount in Matthew 5? Would He have created a web site with key theological points outlined? Would Jesus have a voice mailbox? Would Jesus have performed miracles via digital video and downloaded them on His web site for the entire world to see? I don't think so.

Synergy is what the disciples and Jesus had a handle

on thousands of years before the word was defined (Luke 6:13). They knew what chemistry would do if they hitched their team together. Jesus ate meals, slept, taught, trained, suffered, laughed, and experienced real life with His men on a day-in, day-out basis. This is why they believed so much in Him as the Messiah, which was prophesied by their forefathers (John 2:11). Can you imagine if Jesus had bought into our western culture these beliefs and discipled His men by correspondence? It was for this very reason that Jesus refused to send His disciples out to set up churches and preach the good news alone. He always sent them out two by two just as the animals Noah took on the Ark came in. In this Techno World in which we live, we are riding dangerously close to the mountains edge if we think ministry and the gospel can be effectively transmitted in isolation. I'm not saying God can't use the radio, Internet or cell phones, yet I am saying if that's your only means, you've missed a very important teaching dynamic that Jesus modeled. Jesus was "with" His people using real life teachable moments to transfer truth.

How do we maintain "synergy" in our homes, businesses, churches, and teams? What can we glean from the life of Christ as a formula for success? I believe it begins with a reconstruction of reality in our distorted lenses so we can see from the perspective of God. We all need to come to the conclusion that there is more power in numbers and than individualism. A practical way to avoid this trap is to swallow our independent pride and position ourselves for success interdependently. Focus our attention and efforts on those around us, in our circles, which we might benefit from hitching up to. Scripture is clear that if a house is divided it WILL fall (Luke 11:17). Examine our life and see where we are running alone and how we might rejoin the herd for strength. The results will be monumental!

21

Choosing Your Mountains

Just what exactly is a priority? Who defines what is a priority? What are the consequences for bad prioritizing? These are all questions that leaders deal with every waking moment of a day. I glean some of the greatest words of wisdom from the wisest person I know, my wife. I have heard her tell others, and model to everyone, that one of the keys in this life is learning how to, "Choose your mountains."

If you have energy to burn and a little time on your hands, you need to come to Colorado and climb a Fourteener. A Fourteener is a mass of mountain that stretches heavenward above 14,000 feet. The third hardest mountain to climb in Colorado is Long's Peak. Now if you want to conquer the extreme, just load you up a pack, get you some good hiking shoes and ascend. You will see scenery you've never seen before, outdoor life rarely captured on film, and breath the cleanest air in North America. Climbing one of these mountains is not for the faint of heart though.

When it comes to prioritizing, make sure the heaviest weight is below the water surface so your boat doesn't turn over. Everyone comes face to face with making a decision to either claim a circumstance as a mountain or a molehill. The decision is yours, how do you accumulate data to make the choice? What process do you go through to categorize certain happenings? In this chapter I will either convince you of a plan or confuse you to death. Hopefully I'll do the first.

If you're an attorney, priority is a legal precedence in exercise of rights over the same subject matter. If you're a leader, it means to list or rate projects or goals in a certain order. In other words prioritizing means something meriting prior attention. As a leader you are faced with lots of life-changing decisions everyday. You decide whom to hire, fire, encourage, train, delegate to, and reprove. You decide what happens, when it happens, and where it happens.

The million-dollar question is from where does the meriting come? The answer is, your values. If you value your career over your family then guess who feels like a molehill? If you value your leisure over your job, then guess who pays? If you value your feelings over the facts, guess what wins? I think you see my point here; your priorities are in direct relation to who you are and who you are dictates what you choose to invest your time in. Time is the best barometer for indicating what a person's priorities really are. Priorities answer what price you're going to pay.

The way you rate a list of to-dos is a reflection of what you appreciate in your life the most. If you're selfish, then your priorities will be slanted towards you. If your self-image is not healthy, then your priorities will lean towards what feeds your self-worth. There are those priorities we all have to do that we wish we didn't. Maybe it's a meeting or appointment, a paper or presentation to prepare, a trip you have to make, speech you have to give, or a debt you have to pay. Whatever the case, we all put ourselves in jobs or circumstances that require prioritization.

Make your first priority each day to, "Love your God" (Duet. 6:5). You do this by filling your spiritual tank each morning by getting to know Him through Bible study and prayer. This will help you throughout the day's events as you prioritize the high and low priorities. Next, if you're married, make your spouse a priority by your words and actions. The first social institution invented by God was the institute of marriage. Dating is not just what you do until you get married, date your mate weekly. When you come home from work each day, be ready when you hit the door to help with supper, clean dishes, vacuum, tutor the kids, clean the house and fold laundry. I know this doesn't look like the, "Typical" modern-day man but leave it up to Hollywood to devalue the image. If you have children, show them they are a priority by spending time with them and being involved with their lives more than a weeks vacation each year. Whether you have boys, girls or both, put on your to-do list a date each week with each one individually. Get involved with a body of believers for fun and fellowship with the like-minded. Make valuable relationships a priority by phone calls, notes and meetings. After all this is done, make your career a priority by working hard and making the most out of the time you're there. Don't waste time on the company's nickel. Be a worker that is available, teachable and dependable.

When it comes to the final word of what your priorities will be, you're the judge. How about the use of your time as you define your priorities? Do you have control of it? Because if you don't, someone else will, someone who doesn't have your priority system. God will not interfere but He will honor or discard your ways. Keep in mind the end result of what you do and when you do them. Be conscience of the image of leadership you are portraying to those that are watching you. May it be a Godly, not a worldly one. Leadership is like juggling different aspects of your life. Your career is a rubber ball but your family and friends are glass balls. You drop your career it will bounce back, drop your family and friends, they break. Be a leader who know which mountains are worth the effort and time. Balance is everything!

22

Solitude

It's normally around mid-November that the high country mountain streams begin to freeze and will remain so until mid-April to early May. The flow of the streams is reduced dramatically by the grip of winter, and the trout inhabiting the streams seek out deep holes containing enough water for them to survive until the spring meltdown. The fish become very dormant in the numbing water and they remain in what appears to be suspended animation without even eating. Come spring, the warmer waters swell the rivers and streams and the trout are as good as new and ready for a new season.

How we as humans fight that period of inactivity! I know God leads us into periods of solitude, which can be very uncomfortable. As men, so much of our identity can be tied directly to what and how much we do. I've spent much of my life functioning as a human "doing" and not a human "being." If it wasn't for "doing," I wasn't earning my right "to be." People described me as a, "do-to-be" legalistic striving for my self-worth and identity. When God created Adam, he breathed into the nostrils and the dirt became a human "being." Being what? Being in love with God. God calls you to slow down, jump off the treadmill of life, and "be still" (Psalms 46:10). God calls us all, especially those who set themselves apart as leaders, to rest for a season [period of time], for their own good. The prophet Isaiah says, "Those who wait upon the Lord will gain NEW strength; they will mount up with wings like eagles" (40:31). Each person needs to determine what that period of solitude needs to look like, based on personal self-evaluation and outside Godly counsel. The issue is never "If" you need time of solitude. The issue is when are you going to schedule it?

Our western culture applauds work-a-holics and over-doers. Even our Christian communities encourage this because it looks as if you are "doing" for God and paints the illusion of spiritual usefulness. NOT! God cares far more about who you are than what you do for Him. Jesus spent 30 years of solitude and preparation for his ministry and just 3 years of "doing." In our Christian culture today, we take an unexperienced seminary graduate, immature Christian musician or athlete and thrust them into the world's spotlight to represent God. Read the Sermon on the Mount in Matthew chapters 5-7 and see if chapter 5 doesn't address internal character issues first. During Jesus' ministry, He would leave the multitudes and head for the hills for some solo solitude to get his spiritual batteries recharged. God's not going to do what you can do anyway; He's going to do what you can't do!

What stops you from times of aloneness? Why do you do what you do? Is it to, "Pay God back" or a, "Down payment" to get a luxury room reservation in heaven? What should be done during a time of solitude? Let me offer a few suggestions:

1) *Pray*: Praise (Ps. 100:4), singing hymns, thanksgiving, repentance (1 John 1:9), petitions for others (2 Chronicles 7:14; 1 Timothy 2:8).

2) *Fast*: Juice, water (Luke 2:37; Acts 13:3; Matt. 6:16).

3) *Journal*: What your learning (Eph. 1:13).

4) *Listen*: To what God might be saying to you through the "Still moments." Listen to a CD or tape of praise and worship music (Psalms 29:2; 95:6; Phil 2:10).

5) *Read*: God's Word "intently," Psalms 33:4 [Take an expository and Bible word dictionary], meditate on what you read (Joshua 1:8).

*Warnings: Stay away from self-help books. Cleanse yourself and purify your mind with God's Holy Word (Jer. 22:29).

The goal of time away from the hustle and bustle in solitude is to refocus, redirect and recharge. 1 Peter 4:8 says, "Keep fervent in your love for one another." When scripture asks the followers of Christ to be "fervent" in their love, it means: to be stretched out like a runner trying to win the race at the finish line. We have a lost pagan society in the dark and we're not painting a convincing picture to them that a life apart from a relationship with Christ is a loss. We do this by remaining connected to our Lord and unified as a body. How are you doing? When is your next season of solitude? Where? Is it on your top priority list?

23

Crisis

It was not what I would deem a typical day on September 10, 1991 at 3:30pm on a hot sunny afternoon in Branson, Missouri. I was working as a director at Kanakuk Kamps when I was buzzed on the intercom by my secretary with the message "Hurry home Kyle, your house is on fire." Now, what would you do with a message like that? I reacted as most men would and suppressed my initial reaction of bone chilling fear with a cool response, "I'll be out of the office the rest of the day so hold all calls." My office was only a few minutes away and I jumped into my Jeep and scurried quickly towards home. We had just built this 4200 sq. ft. ranch style home about 18 months earlier on an acre of property surrounded by Cedar trees in the Ozark Mountains. My wife and I had designed this home for two years and wanted to build what every couple with young children wants, their "Dream Home." It had vaulted ceilings, spacious kitchen, 5 roomy bedrooms, hot tub and a wrap around covered porch. As I rounded the corner about 100 yards from my driveway I looked up and saw smoke rising up about 500 feet. Obviously, this was no kitchen grease fire. It was a fully engulfing fire that was consuming every square inch of our new home. The town in which we resided was Branson, MO, and the fire department was staffed by a bunch of thrown together volunteers with little experience, which I happen to have been one of them. It will amaze you how you will react under extreme crisis and chaos. I did a Starsky and Hutch power-slide in my Jeep, saw my wife freaking out, then I ran inside the burning house looking for my 2 1/2 year old son. Daniel's bedroom was upstairs and he always took his afternoon nap from 3-4:30pm. After about dying of smoke inhalation and my clothes partially catching on fire, I came to the conclusion he wasn't in the house and neither should I be. After my fellow fire fighters arrived, the house was a total loss including the new mini-van parked in the garage. We had lost everything we owned and all we now owned were the clothes on our backs and an old Jeep. We had no money, no toothbrush, no place to sleep, no soap, no shoes, no nothing, yet life was simple. That night, as I reflected on the nightmare, hoping to wake up and have it be just that, I realized how very fortunate I was not to have lost my wife and child in the fire. God revealed to me how very lucky I really was.

I share this story to set a precedent that crisis plays no favorites. As a leader, you have to be involved with people or you aren't leading. With the element of human beings you will always have some sort of crisis to face. Whether individually or corporately, the tornado is coming your way. How do you handle those moments of crisis? Do those you lead look to you for a model of stability or an example of panic in an earth suit? As a leader, you need to anticipate that trials and tribulation will come (James 1:2). The old saying, "An ounce of prevention is worth a pound of cure" is good but theologically unsound. Just because you are prepared doesn't mean that it's going to stop crisis from happening.

Moses handled crisis after crisis and you must ask, how did he do it? He went to the Lord for guidance and wisdom. Solomon needed an extra- strength dose of wisdom and he ask God for it and got it. Jonah prayed for help in a whale's belly, Joshua listened to the Lord's counsel, young David looked to the Lord to help his rock find the forehead of a giant, Esther prayed for protection in the midst of crisis, Hannah prayed for a child, Job prayed for perspective, Isaiah asked for clean lips, Jeremiah prayed not to bypass the judgment but to have strength to endure it, Jesus looked to His Father for direction and strength.

The common tread through all these leaders was that they knew from where their direction should come, God! 1 Corinthians 16:13 tells us to, "Be on the alert, stand firm in the faith and act like men, be strong." Philippians 4:6 says for leaders to be, "Anxious for nothing but in prayer, and supplication, let your requests be made known to God." In other words, find Christ in the crisis. He is there with you and for you. In the Shepherd's Psalm chapter 23 you remember the part that says, "Even though I walk through the valley of the shadow of death I shall fear no evil for Thou art with me?" Can't you see that our awesome God of light is with you in the low times of crisis. That's why there is a shadow. As a leader you first must seek God's face in every circumstance you encounter. I realize this sounds so elementary and old fashioned but it's true and it works. You need to seek God on the mountaintop of success and in the valley of turmoil. God is not a rescue boat that is only used when your ship is sinking. He's not a 911 God. He is a jealous God that desires relation (Ex. 20:5).

In conclusion, we all are going to make mistakes but the question is do we learn from those times? In a crisis, you're not going to always respond the right way but do you refer to God for help? Don't get caught by surprise or feel alone when crisis comes knocking at your door. Leaders all over the world are facing crisis and trying hard to be a sturdy Palm Tree that bends but doesn't break in midst of the Hurricanes of leadership. Look for Christ in the crisis! He won't do what you can do. He'll only do what He can do and that's why He waits anxiously for the prayers of the helpless. Give Him a call soon.

24

Significance

Do you know the difference between a, "Pipe" and a "Pump?" One allows something to flow through. The other is the source. As a leader, which of the two items are you? Are you the origin or a passageway for truth? A Godly leader is a pipe because they see the value of transferring instead of being the originator.

As a "Pipe," our relationship on a daily basis with the living God is of paramount importance if we are going to please Him in our leadership methods. This relationship will look like seeking God's direction through the Holy Spirits guidance, through prayer, and in every step we take and decision we make. As a leader, every decision we make, including those we make subconsciously, has got to honor God. In Psalms 32:8 you will see that we gain and glean this truth as a leader from the scriptures, "I will instruct you and teach you in the way that you should go; I will guide you with my eye."

As a leader who is more responsible before God, our strength and significance has got to originate from God. There is nothing, absolutely nothing, that should replace a daily meeting with God as you learn His leadership secrets and His significance through the Word of God, prayer and walking in obedience to His revealed will to us. This relationship is a vital necessity for effective Christian Leadership.

Finding daily significance in my relationship with Jesus Christ is what allows me as leader to pursue excellence. Dr. John Gardner says, "The society which scorns excellence in plumbing because plumbing is a humble activity, and tolerates shoddiness in philosophy because it is an exhausted activity, will have neither good plumbing nor good philosophy. Neither its pipes nor its theories will hold water." Colossians 3:23 is a life verse I work by and played sports by for years. It reminds me comparison is carnality, "Whatever you do, do it heartily for the Lord and not for men." The question here is who is your audience? Your boss, family, fellow employees, players, students? It needs to be the God of the heavens as your main spectators because He is where you draw your approval and significance rating from—by your heart not your performance. Dr. Schaffer the founder of Dallas Seminary once said: "There is nothing you can ever do that will cause God to love you more. Nothing you can do to cause God to love you less." Are you content on what you're becoming as leader? Check first where you draw your significance. Dr. Mel Lorentzen reminds us that, "We must stress excellence over mediocrity done in the name of Christ. We must determine to put our best into the arts, so that when we sing a hymn about Jesus' love, when we erect a building for the worship of God, when we stage a play about the soul's pilgrimage, we will not repel people, but attract them to God." King Solomon wrote, "Whatever your hand finds to do, do it with all your might." The apostle Paul's encouraging words in Philippians 1: 9 are most appropriate: "It is my prayer that your love may abound more and more, with knowledge and all discernment, so that you may prove what is excellent, and may be pure and blameless for the day of Christ, filled with the fruits of righteousness which come through Jesus Christ, to the glory and praise of God."

To pursue excellence in our service is not the pursuit of a life style; it is not the pursuit of education; it is not the pursuit of money. Excellence is the pursuit of Christ. If we want to be excellent, we need to seek to be like the Excellent One! Remember, excellence is never an accident. As a leader that pursues excellence, you will attract others who desire the same. We don't attract what we aren't. Be a leader who draws your significance from your personal relationship with Jesus Christ.

There is a true story about a Romanian pastor of a small underground Christian church named Tshang. The story was that this pastor was supposed to be shot by the KGB as they stormed his study in his home where he was reading his Bible and praying one day. As they kicked down the door, machine guns equipped, and confronted Tshang, he told them, "Go ahead and shoot me as ordered. Then my followers will wonder why I died for the cause of Christ." Your self-worth and significance as a leader should come from your Savior, only.

25

Mentoring

If you ask ten people the question, you'll get 10 different answers. What exactly is mentoring? The Greek word for teaching means: student is passive, in a learning position. The Hebrew word for teaching is based more on relationship, experience, and is transformational. The correct English definition is: A lifelong relationship where the mentor helps the protégé reach his or her God-given potential in life. Mentoring is like a faithful Clydesdale draft horse. Why? Racehorses are there for the short sprint; Clydesdales are there for the long haul. The mentoring process is exactly that, a process that takes T.I.M.E. Mentoring is done in a relationship with someone you like [a natural chemistry exists], trust, believe in (2 Tim. 2:2), and want to see succeed in life's arena's. Mentoring "intentionalizes" a relationship and maturity is the focus. A mentor helps you mature in the vital areas of life.

As we continue to define what exactly mentoring looks like in the 21st Century, we need to say what it is not. It is not a fancy form of evangelism or a plan of discipleship. The evangelist's agenda is the gospel, the discipler's agenda is spiritual disciplines and the mentor's agenda is goals and problems. The apostle Paul was an evangelist who discipled Timothy yet Barnabas was Paul's mentor. Barnabas was consistent, fun, trustworthy, affirming, saw potential in Paul and accepted him as he was. Sound like a good quality for a mentor? Mentors don't have to be as old as dirt. They aren't perfect or have all the answers to life's puzzling questions...they're there for the journey and to help and counsel when and where they can. Speaking into the life of a protégé is learned; speaking with authority is earned!

A textbook of scripture example is Barnabas who sold all he had in Cyprus and came to Jerusalem to give it all to the church. Barnabas later came to Saul [Paul] after his dramatic touch by Ananias where the scales on Paul's eyes fell off on the Damascus road experience and Barnabas mentored Paul along in his faith. None of the church leaders in Jerusalem wanted anything to do with Paul for fear of his past temper and persecution of fellow Christians. If it weren't for Barnabas, who knows what Paul would have done next. In Acts 9:26-27 you'll find a description of how Barnabas took Saul to the apostles and talked his way into the fellowship of the apostles. That's not the end though; Barnabas later traveled with Paul spreading the good news (Acts 13:13) and confronted him about how he treated John Mark (Acts 15:36-38). So even though we know today how important and influential the Apostle Paul was in the New Testament, don't forget the man behind the stallion.

How important is mentoring? Well let's just see. If you're a numbers person, let me show you some math. If you mentored in your lifetime 12 folks who then went on to mentor 12, you would have influenced 144 people. Now if those 144 mentored 12, you'd have 1,728. Of those, if they each took on 12 protégés, you'd have 20,236 and then 248,832 to have a grand total of 2,985,984 people you influenced in your life for Christ! Talk about being an impact player for God. You never know exactly what the Lord may do with your protégé. Who knows, you may be mentoring a Billy Graham, Elizabeth Elliott, Jim Dobson, Mother Teresa, Abe Lincoln and not even know it. When you influence a child, you influence a life. When you influence a parent, you influence an entire family. When you influence a president you influence a corporation. When you influence a pastor, you influence a church. When you influence a leader, you influence all who look to him or her for leadership. We are so many Paul's looking for a Barnabas to link us back to our past and steer us to our future. Mentoring is the relational glue that can hold our generation to the past and to the future. Mentoring is the relational bridge connecting, strengthening, and stabilizing future generations of believers. Protégés are those teachable, eager souls for whom God places in our hearts a lifelong love. Protégés need us as their mentors to love them (1 John 4:18), challenge them, guide them, and introduce them to our closest friends with pride as a, "lifelong friend!" A senior citizen can mentor a mature adult. A mature adult can mentor a young adult. A young adult can mentor a college student. A college student can mentor a high school student. A high school student can mentor a junior higher. Anyone can, but not everyone should become a mentor.

Here are some thoughts and questions on how to choose YOUR protégé:

Do you believe in them?
How is the chemistry between you?
Do you like their family?
Do you trust them?
Are they F.A.T.? [Faithful; available and teachable]
Do they respect and admire you?
Are they proactive and self motivated?
Are they comfortable and natural with you?
Are they worth your investment of time?
Now pray for discernment but remember, in seeking
    a protégé, don't hesitate, initiate!

If you're a protégé looking for a mentor, here are some questions to ask before you make your choice:

Are they honest with you?
Are they a role model? Spiritually; physically; socially;
    intellectually.
Do they get emotionally "naked" with you? Are they
    open and transparent?
Are they a person who is committed to you?
Do they see potential in you?
Do they know your dreams and can they help you
    make those into reality?
Are they successful in your definition?
Are they humble enough to learn from you as you are
    learning from them?

Are they willing to focus on your agenda more than their own?

*Note: Accountability is from God and just because a mentor lets you get by with something doesn't mean God will.

There is a hassle to mentoring but it's worth it. Listen to these wise words Paul writes to Timothy in 2 Timothy 2:2, "And the things which you have received from me, entrust these things to faithful men who are able to teach others." Do you see how you can leave a legacy behind after you are gone, rather than leaving behind a bunch of stink? There is a risk, that's why few do it. Remember though…you've got to go out on a limb to get the best fruit! The late great coach of the Dallas Cowboys Tom Landry once said, "I just hope that when it's all over, that I've helped some people have a better life because they have know me somewhere along the way. I don't care if I'm in the Hall of Fame or whether I'm remembered for any reason other than that." Laborers can't be massed produced; they must be raised up through life on life mentoring. Success, without a successor, is failure. Just like the Apostle Paul, we ALL need a special "Touch" by someone in our lives. You've got your marching orders; go touch somebody!

26

Accountability

Hebrews 10:24 says, "Let us [you] consider how to spur [irritate] one another on to love and good deeds." Several years ago when I was young and stupid I took on the rough and tumble sport of rodeo as a hobby. I grew up in Texas with a father who raised and trained high-spirited racehorses, but never did I have the desire to try rodeo. I always say, "If your gonna be a bear, be a Grizzly, not a Panda." I was 23 years old when I started going to Lyle Sankey Christian Rodeo Schools in Abbyville, Kansas to learn the "Rough stock" side of pro rodeo as a bull rider. I lived with Lyle [4-time PRCA World Champion Rodeo star] and his wife Kathy for two years in a log cabin in the Ozark Mountains in southwest Missouri and traveled some with Lyle to rodeos around the country. To be honest, I was long on toughness but short on ability in this pro sport. In other words, the 1200-pound bulls won most of the battles. I loved watching Lyle on a saddle bronc horse spurring the fire out of these animals and looking like he was going to get bucked right out of the arena. I asked Lyle why he spurred the horse when they bucked hard enough without that irritation. His answer was Biblical, "The drag of the spurs pulls me back down in my saddle and irritates the horse enough to get him to perform better than it would without the irritation."

We all need cheerleaders in our life. We need someone who motivates us and encourages us to be better than we would be without them. Who asks you, "Are ya' clean?" Who irritates you with motives to build you up to be a better man or woman and challenges those times you lie, gossip, or quit? Confrontation is right only when the offense is in direct opposition to scripture. The attitude you have when confronting will be more important than the words you speak. Who spurs you on to a deeper commitment to your family, your God and your occupation? Pastor Adrian Rodgers answered when asked what's wrong with churches in America? He replied, "I've never seen a group like the church that negotiates commitment," discipleship made easy. Commitment doesn't come easy, we need a cheerleader to help us in this critical area of life. When you get someone to hold you accountable to love and good deeds, I recommend someone who loves you deeply, knows you well, and is not impressed easily. I have two gray haired men named Bob Howey and Stan Holmes who I meet with regularly to hold me accountable to being the man of God I'm meant to be. They spur me on to stay faithful and active in my marriage and as a dad. I suggest you get men who are older, mature in their faith, married many years to one wife and have kids who aren't perfect but respectful and giving back to society in a positive form (1 Tim. 3:1-7). Here are some questions I have my accountability partners ask me when we meet.

Accountability questions: (2 Peter 1:10)

Have you been spending daily time in the scriptures and prayer?

Have you had any flirtations or lustful thoughts, attitudes or temptations?

Have you exposed yourself to any explicit materials [movies; magazines; internet], which would not glorify God?

Have you been completely above reproach in your financial dealings?

Have you spent quality time with your kids, wife, and good friends?

How have you loved your wife like Christ loves the church?

Have you told any half-truths or lies, putting yourself in a better light to those around you?

Have you shared the gospel with an unbeliever this week?

Have you taken care of your body through physical exercise, proper eating, and sleeping habits?

Have you allowed any person or circumstance to rob you of your joy?

Have you encouraged anyone recently? Who?

Have you been totally truthful in your answering the above questions?

Note: Critical areas you need accountability in are: home life, work life, spiritual life.

Proverbs 27:17 says, "Iron sharpens iron, so one man sharpens another." You're not any closer to hell if sparks are flying but it's good to yoke yourself with someone who will chip away at your rough edges. Be transparent and vulnerable, keeping what is said confidential. Just as in mentoring, you need trust, chemistry and loyalty to make accountability a viable, working tool for personal and spiritual growth. Never forget the purpose of accountability: To each day become more Christ-like in all of your ways. Remember it is Jesus who is the object of our search, our devotion, our sacrifices, and our affection. Anything less than intimacy with the living Lord will be a waste of your time together.

Accountability is for a quiet time, praying for and with each other, confessing your sins to one another (James 5:16), and accountability for your actions and attitudes. Some of the advantages of accountability are that you will be less likely to stumble and fall. Accountability is not a perfect system but you will be more likely to see the big picture and not as likely to "get away" with sin. Accountability includes: vulnerability, teachability, availability and honesty. Remember you are accountable to God, your spouse, and your accountability partners. Accountability is trusting your life to someone you have carefully selected who lives above reproach (Phil. 2:15). They have the right to examine you and your lifestyle, the right to question you, the right to reprove you, and the right to give you Godly counsel. Be proactive in finding an accountability partner who will fill these shoes. What are you waiting on?

27

Money and Materialism

Did you know that the Bible talks more about money and materialism than it does heaven or hell? What is this? What is it about the all mighty dollar that draws such divine attention? Let me set the record straight at the beginning of the chapter, money and stuff are not the issue, the love of money and stuff is the issue (1 Tim. 3:3 and 6:10). The richest man ever, King Solomon, warns those who think the almighty dollar is the answer to all of life's questions, "Those that love money will NOT be satisfied" (Eccl. 5:10). Now this is a man who was told no to nothing. I have an acquaintance that is a multi-billionaire who is imprisoned by his wealth. Everywhere he goes and every person he meets with has the undertones of money, power and wealth. I heard a gambler in Reno once answer the question, how much is enough? His reply, "Just one more dollar."

Everything in your home is either an idol or a tool. We live in the most materialistic, debt-ridden culture in the universe. The average American home has at least eight credit cards at their disposal. We buy stuff we don't need, with money we don't have, to impress people we don't like. I grew up in a community in Dallas that was, and still is, very materialistic. What mattered was the car you drove, the purse you carried, the designer labels on your clothes, the square footage of your house, the country club you belonged to, the school your kids went to, and the places you vacation. From the outside it looks like a dog chasing its tail. What matters to God has very little to do, in fact no relation to image and prosperity. Our communities have so many "dual" income [both parents work full-time] families supposedly because that is what it takes to live. My first question to those couples with children at home would be why? To pay for the necessities of life or the toys? My next question would be to define for me your definition of needs verses wants? Our culture has a distorted reality of this definition. If you were to ask ten different people you likely will get ten different answers. What I mean by that is our definitions are skewed due to our upbringing and the environment in which we live. Third World countries would define *need* a bit different than we would I'm sure. I am NOT saying that dual income families or working mothers are Biblically wrong unless the motives and reasons are wrong. God promises He will supply all our needs: food, shelter and clothing [Phil 4:19]. Did you know that every time Jesus used the phrase "Ye of little faith" [Matt. 6:30] it was in response to doubting that God would fulfill His promises when it dealt with their food, shelter, clothing or in reference to span of life?

As a leader, we need to rise above the standard, the norm, the socially accepted. Don't get yourself caught in the rat race of chasing that which will wither and tarnish.

"Stuff" will not gain you more happiness or fill a void in your life. All that we will accumulate on this earth will not get you favor with God or get you into eternity. Have you ever seen a U-Haul behind a hearse? I realize we are in a system that requires money but are you entrapped by the system? There is nothing wrong with making, giving, investing or spending money, but when it becomes your idol, you step out of use and into idolatry worship. Realize its God's and not yours. The Lord's Prayer makes it clear who is the ultimate provider, "Give us this day our daily bread." Here are a few tips for a leader when it comes to money:

Understand the grip [love] of money and materialism.

Give regularly to the poor and needy. It helps keep perspective.

Don't flaunt that which God has allowed you to possess.

Steer clear of envy and petty jealousies over stuff and status.

Operate within your means.

Don't over leverage yourself. [Spending or living beyond your income].

Stay out of debt when at all possible.

2 Corinthians 4:18 says, "While we look not at the things seen, but at the things which are not seen; for the things which are seen are temporal, but the things which

are not seen are eternal." Have you ever wondered why Fortune 500 pays their top executives so much money? Because they've got the answer. Leadership makes the difference! As a husband and father, your leadership makes a difference in your family. Your family might be able to survive from day to day but are they heading anywhere? Are they growing in Christ-like character and focusing in on what matters? There is little argument about the fact that marriages and families are in trouble. Too many men are functioning only as material providers. In our country, we need a "new breed" of men who will focus in on the spiritual aspect of their family life. We need a new breed of men who have the ability to focus on the unseen, the eternal, as well as the seen. Men who will say "no" to more bucks when it comes to sacrificing their families. Men who ask before they do, "How will this affect the relationships within my family?" New men who will recognize they need to leave something to posterity that will outlive the financial inheritances they may leave for their kids like proven character. This new breed of men recognizes that to succeed in the eyes of men but fail in the eyes of God is the ultimate failure. It is said, "It is better to fail in a cause that will ultimately succeed than to succeed in a cause that will ultimately fail."

Will you take upon yourself the challenge Albert Einstein gave a group of young highly motivated scientists, "Gentlemen, try not to become men of success. But rather, try to become men of value."

28

Core Values

The following chart illustrates how we learn. Notice the most effective learning occurs through experience. Note the top four are mass communication and the last six are individuals and small groups. Increase levels of learning broaden as you move from top to bottom.

Verbal symbols-words
Visual symbols- charts, graphs, maps
Radio, recordings, still pictures
Motion pictures
Exhibits
Field trips
Demonstrations
Dramatic presentations- observation-participation
Contrived experiences
Direct experiences

Determining your CORE values:

What do you believe in?

What really matters to you?

What values help you govern the way you live your life?

What values do you want to pass on to your children?

I find that most leaders make decisions according to a few "core values." But many leaders have never taken the time to articulate just what those values are. If you want to leave a godly legacy, you first must determine what you believe in, what is most important to you. Then you need to evaluate how well you are living according to those values, because your children will learn from your actions and lifestyle more than your words. For example, if one of your core values is, "my family comes before my job," and your kids see you consistently working so many hours that you rarely have time to spend with them, they will conclude that your real core value is, "My work is more important than my family."

What are your core values in your family, church, company, team, or in your classroom today?

What do you want to pass down to your kids, employees, students as far a core values?

How well does your lifestyle reflect these values? Pull out a calendar and see how your schedule reflects those values?

How does your mate's or co-workers values complement you as you raise a family or run an organization?

How are your teammates, employees, church staff, family members values similar? Different?

Where do you need unity in your workplace, family, church, etc.?

Spiritual values: Do you as a leader?
Trust Christ as Savior and Lord
Love God with all your heart
Have child-like faith
Believe the Bible is truth
Have a tender heart
Have a forgiving spirit
Are you full of hope and joy
Are you submissive or stubborn
Believe in the power of prayer
Do you love others
Treat your wife like Christ treats the church
Respect your husband

Civic and cultural values: Do you or are you?
Obey the law and authority
Are you patriotic
Do you have convictions about specific issues
Are you social minded

Relational values: As a leader, are you?
Caring
Kind
Giving or stingy
Generous
Merciful
Gracious
Friendly
Team player
Compassionate
Respectful of others' views, ideas, opinions, interests
Helpful/Serving

Allow me to wrap this up. What exactly do you stand for? If I were to interview your co-workers, employees, churchgoers, teammates, students, family, what would they say are your core values? Values are evident and visible in the way we manage our affairs and behave. Make for yourself, family, company, church, team or whatever arena you lead, a mission statement that states who you are and what you stand for. There is a old country song with a chorus that says, "You've got to stand for something or you'll fall for anything." Stand for Truth or sit down!

29

Personal Growth

I am, to put it mildly, an avid fly fisherman which is not hard to be when you live in beautiful Colorado. The scriptures tells us that through creation all mankind will know of God's divine nature and eternal power. As an outdoorsman, this makes sense to me yet still I'm surprised daily how God chooses to impact a precept in my own life. As a stream-inhabiting fish, the Rainbow Trout has only one choice about his position: he must face the oncoming current of the water. If he turns his tail on the current too long, the force of the rushing water will fill his gills and he will drown. At the very least, he would be swept down stream where there would be a rigorous effort of regaining lost distance.

It is a strategic ploy of the enemy, the devil, to get us as leaders to turn downstream. If he can get us to turn and look and live in our past, he can rob us of our present and future hope that lies ahead of us. Paul supports this position in Philippians 3:13 where he says to, "Forget about the past and strain toward what is ahead." This is not to say we can't learn from the past, it's just that we can't live in it nor find fulfillment there. Facing upstream means facing reality, and reality is found in the present and future provisions of a loving Lord.

Sitting by a mountain stream and watching a trout feed in a stream is fascinating. If you want to catch a silly fish, the first thing you need to do before you go to Orvis and unload your pocket book is study their feeding habits. A trout will seek out a, "feeding lane" and WILL NOT move from it, no matter how many feeding opportunities pass by. I have seen these fish ignore an insect as well as my dry-fly lures as they floated only a few inches to the right or left of the feeding lane. Trout are programmed to feed in lanes for a specific reason. If they went darting around the stream after every insect they saw, they could become seriously calorie deficient. Just because a tempting morsel floats by doesn't mean its suppertime.

I think of how many times talented people and leaders try to consume every opportunity they see and overload themselves. I have struggled with this challenge for years because I rationalized all the opportunities were orchestrated by my loving heavenly Father as a gift to me, His son. Boy howdy, did I misread those opportunities. Your "feeding lane" is narrow by design. In the center you are to focus on Christ and it is there you will find your healthy provision. To your right and left could lay opportunities that will sink you. Don't you know that after Peter sank in the sea while walking toward Jesus on the water that on his way back to the boat he never took his eyes off Christ? Your vision needs to be straight upstream, in the center of your divinely designed feeding lane. God's advice to a young leader of the people of Israel as he led them to the Promise Land was, "Don't look to the right or left so you will have success wherever you go." (Joshue 1:7). The wisest king in scripture, Solomon, advises the same in Proverbs 4:25-27, "Let your eyes look straight ahead, fix your gaze directly before you." Attractions to your right or left can distract, tempt and ultimately destroy you, just ask Peter.

There was once a Shakespearean actor who was known everywhere for his one-man shows, readings and recitations from the classics. He would always end his performance with a dramatic reading of Psalm 23. Each night, without exception, as the actor is doing his recitation- "The Lord is my Shepherd, I shall not want" the crowd would listen attentively. And then, at the conclusion of the Psalm, they would rise in thunderous applause in appreciation of the actor's incredible ability to bring the verse to life. One night, just before the actor was to offer his customary recital of Psalms 23, a young man from the audience spoke up. "Sir, do you mind if tonight I recite Psalms 23?" the actor was quite taken back by this unusual request, but he allowed the young man to come forward and stand in front and center stage to recite the Psalm, knowing that the ability of his unskilled youth would be no match for his talent. With a soft voice, the young man began to recite the words of the Psalm. When he was finished, there was no applause. There was no standing ovation as on other nights. All that could be heard was the sound of weeping. The audience had been so moved by the young man's recitation that there was not a dry eye in the house. Amazed by what he heard and saw, the actor said to the young man, "I don't understand. I have been performing Psalms 23 for years. I have a lifetime of experience and training but I have never been able to move an audience as you have tonight. Tell me, what is your secret?" The young man replied, "Well sir, you know the Psalm; I know the Shepherd." Do you know all the Christian ways, clichés and means of acting out the parts of modern day Christianity or do you really KNOW Him? If not, get to know Him by staying focused forward (Heb. 12:2) in your spiritual feeding lane. Make a daily priority to find a quiet place to read, study, pray, and meditate on the Holy Scriptures. Feed your spiritual soul before you feed your physical stomach.

30

Failure

Victor Frankl is quoted as saying, "Not having a goal is more to be feared than not reaching a goal. I would rather attempt to do something great and fail than attempt nothing and succeed." You can tell the success of a leader by the number of failures he or she has had. One of my favorite quotes in my office is by Theodore Roosevelt, "The credit belongs to the man who is actually in the arena-his face is marred by dust, sweat, and blood...who knows the great enthusiasm, the great devotion, and spends himself in a worthy cause. Who at best if he wins knows the thrill of high achievement-and if he fails at least fails while daring greatly-so that his place shall never be with those cold and timid souls who knows neither victory or defeat."

Peter the Apostle failed and it was recorded in scripture. He denied Jesus not once, but three times before the cock crowed. His failure was recorded four different times in the world's best-selling book, the Bible. Maybe at times, you feel like Peter did on that awful day. You've failed, and you don't know if God will forgive you or could ever use you as a leader again. As a leader, don't give up and quit because of a mishap. As Peter realized, failure does not have to be the end of the book.

Failure is inevitable, but it isn't the end of the world. Failure often creates serious consequences, tough days, damaged relationships, and sleepless nights yet it's not fatal. We all fail! We say the wrong thing, do the wrong things, miss a cue, or make a poor decision. Our kids are hurt, our spouse is angry, our boss is disillusioned. A colleague is let down, the future is jeopardized, the car is dented, and the money is gone. Don't give up. Here are some practical ideas of things to do:

Own up to your failure. Don't blame others or dodge your failure. There may be hard consequences, but your identity, acceptance, and value are still secure. God has said so. In fact, you are as secure as Christ is strong. Secure people are not threatened and can admit they made a mistake, committed an act of thoughtlessness, or made a poor decision—and accept responsibility.

Apologize for your failure. Be willing to say, "I was wrong" and apologize, or "I offended you and I'm very sorry."

Don't overestimate your failure. Your failure is not the end of the world. It's easy to fall into the trap of depression, hopelessness, or dejection at the thought of personal failure. Remember that God is ready to forgive—and forget—your failure. There is nothing you can do that will cause God to love you more than He already loves you. And conversely, there is nothing you can do that will cause God to love you less than he already loves you.

Speak honestly about your failure. Paul said, "when I

am weak, then I am strong" (2 Cor. 12:10). Evaluate your failure and use it to gain spiritual maturity and momentum (2 Cor. 10:5; 7:10; Rom. 7:7-25). Talk to trusted friends to gain their perspective and wisdom on your failure.

Be proactive in your failure. Don't let your failure be a demoralizing, fearful, dark pit. Ask God to help you to use your failures as a training field for your spiritual growth. Learn from Peter as he showed faith when he jumped overboard to swim to where Jesus called his name (John 21:7). He was proactive in his failure and abandoned himself to Christ's forgiveness.

Ask for God's help every morning. Declare to the Lord that you are depending on Him today, not your own resources, intellect, position, power, or gifts. This declaration effectively leaves Him in charge of you and the day's activities. Lets end this chapter with an inspirational speech written years ago that addresses this subject of failure.

"There comes a time, the time in every man's life when he is faced with personal crisis or monumental challenge. At this time, the man discovers what truly exist deep down inside his soul. The will is the backbone of the soul. Great men have dreams, hopes and aspirations; average men do not. It is the strength of will, and the fire of determination blazing inside the soul that leads men to fulfill these dreams, hopes and aspirations. Great men reached deep down inside their soul to accept, fight and conquer any and all challenges. Average men never reach this deep and, therefore, falter and are defeated. Your will, and the amount of intensity and determination with which you meet challenges, has no correlation with size, speed, and or ability. For the strength of the will, the backbone of the soul comes from an inner source, much greater than any on earth for it comes from He who created the earth. The question of battle is not the size of the man in the fight, but rather in the size of the fight in the man. Many men have passed through their lives never having heard nor accepted the challenges of the battles of life, only later to regret their failures. For long after the game has been played, the stadium emptied, the score placed in the record books has the failures of man unwilling to rise to the challenge come back to haunt his soul, the fears of failure, the agony of defeat. Men who rise to the challenge, those who release every ounce of energy, on this strength from within, fight and conquer. These men never know the fear of failure, only the taste of success and the thrill of victory. Along the path of life, in search of our dreams, hopes and aspirations, there are many obstacles, many challenges, many battles. Great men are willing to pay the price for success in victory. The fire within their soul blazes greater, and their will strengthened with each battle, each victory. These men strive to reach their ultimate goal–their dreams. Some men dream things as they are and ask WHY? I have dreams that never were and say Why Not? **"Robert Kennedy"**

Failure is not the end…it's the means!

31

Charisma

Charisma in the Greek language is where we derive the modern word: Charismatic. I wanted to address in this chapter the art of motivating with charisma. I need to preface this chapter with the known fact that there is a plethora of ways to do this. Some of you are the cheerleader type and others use the more docile Tom Landry style yet both get the job done. People can be motivated by money, encouragement, fear, pride, and incentives. Some emotional brakes that stop the motivation factor are childhood suppression and peer pressure. If you're a pastor you're needing ways to move the "body" into action. If you're an employer you're looking for creative ways to up your quality of service, product, and productivity. If you're a parent you want solid formulas for a unified, functional family. If you're a coach you love ideas of how to get the most out of a player and maintain oneness on the team. If you're a teacher, you're trying to find a means to teach information that is applicable.

Howard Hendricks at Dallas Theological Seminary says, "If you're going to bore someone, don't bore them with the Bible." Whatever you do, add a dose of enthusiasm and you will be more successful. Dale Carnegie once said, "The people who go the furthest in life are excited about something." What are you excited about today? What gets you up in the mornings? Socrates said, "Assume a virtue if you want to have it." What virtue do you want to have exemplified in your life? Thomas Edison said, "If all we leave our kids is enthusiasm, we've left them an estate of incalculable value."

Read this quote by John Maxwell:

> "Life is not an intellectual experience. It's an emotional one. It's a feeling experience. We don't communicate with the world with words. Words are a secondary source of communication. We communicate with feelings and attitudes. One of the greatest things you can ever do is get excited today about your life [with Christ] and start to live enthusiastically day after day and your whole world will improve. If you wait to get excited until some lucky outer event happens–guess what? If you wait, what does life do? It waits. And if you hold back until a more appropriate time to get excited, what does life do? It holds back. Listen, if you're going to hold back on your enthusiasm, develop lots of patience, because you are going to wait a long time for an exciting life. When you become an excited person, you have an exciting life. When you get excited about your career, you get an exciting career. When you get excited about a relationship, you will get an exciting relationship."

If you want to change an attitude, start with a change

of behavior. People will more admire attitude than they will appearance. Look at nature itself for a minute. Anything that becomes idle for an extended period of time, everything that stops struggling and remains inactive will rapidly deteriorate. It is, and always will be, a struggle towards the ideal, the constant effort to get higher and further in their life is what develops manhood and character. People will catch the lesson like a cold if they get close to you as a leader with charisma. We all need to hang around enthusiastic folks because we can catch the passion. We've got to believe in what we are doing or no one else will. If I am a Christian, then I must believe in God and that alone should give me purpose in life. I must believe in who God made me and that gives me confidence to be a leader. Leaders need to believe in others and that will give us relationships that last forever. I have got to believe in what I do everyday and that will give me enthusiasm.

There is a giant chasm between a person with a dream and a dreamer. The person with a dream talks little and does a lot. The dreamer delivers a lot of lip service and does very little. Life is really simple in one way. Life is energy itself and it is our use of energy that creates the circumstance of our lives that determines the circumstances we are in now. If your desire is to change lives, and it should be if you're a leader, all we have to do is change our energy. Put a little more energy and excitement into your world and you can be a catalyst of change. If you're bored with your career, a relationship, a marriage, church, a team, and you are not excited about it then no one will benefit. Whatever you're excited about and wherever your passions lie, you WILL attract others to your team effortlessly. The greatest mistake people make is waiting for someone else to come in and build them up and try to get them excited and wanting others to give you joy and give you something to get excited about in life. Life doesn't work that way. The quality of your life is your gift to yourself. So next time you are given a lemon in this unfair world, go to squeezing and make you some lemonade! Life really is what YOU make of it, not what hand you've been dealt.

32

Time Management

Thinking about time, and how you use it, can literally change our lives. God will never give us too much to do, but men will. We so often assign ourselves an overload, but the Lord never does. He knows exactly what He wants for and from each of us. There is plenty of time in His day for those things that are essential for His plan. General Dwight Eisenhower always arranged his affairs so that only the truly important matters came across his desk. Wisely, he discovered that urgency and importance seldom came in the same package. He found that really important matters were seldom urgent, and that the most urgent things were seldom important.

As you the leader look at your day, ask yourself a very important question. Do you spend more time on the truly important things or those things that are just urgent? Are you a reactionary leader who just responds to panic buttons? For us as Christian leaders, there is always going to be a sense of urgency. It comes as standard equipment with the position. Jesus definitely felt the same pressure. That's why he is so easy to relate with, when He said: "I must work the works of Him who has sent me, while it is day; the night comes when no man can work" (John 9:4).

148 A Cut Above

Pioneer missionary Robert Moffatt said: "We shall have all eternity in which to celebrate our victories, but we only have one short hour before the sunset in which to win them." You have got to realize this; time is a measurement, a dimension. Time can scarcely be our problem on this planet. When we look hard at the issue of time and its tricky management, all roads ultimately lead you back to the management of yourself! God has given you time just as He gives us other things like: money, talent, our health, experience, knowledge, education, and skill. He gives us the freedom of choice on how we would like to use it. We can choose family, relationships, personal well being, or spiritual growth as priorities. We need to commit and stay held accountable to God and ourselves on how we spend our time accordingly. We can all always make more money but you have a predetermined allotment of time God has given you here on this earth, and you aren't going to make anymore of that.

We must realize that our lifestyle, the decisions and values that underlie it, are closely related to time management. You can tell a lot about someone by where and how they spend their time. Priorities of time don't lie. Tell me how you spend your time. Let me see your checkbook or credit card statement for the past year; let me see your calendar or daily planner; tell me what books you have read recently and I can pretty darn well tell you the kind of person you are without even knowing you.

God is very clear in His Commandments that he wants all of us, especially leaders, to keep Him No. 1 on the list. If you have a family, you need to spend time with them daily both physically and emotionally [are you there when you're there?]. My wife and kids don't give a rip about quality verses quantity time; they know I care for them because I'm there. Time is one commodity that is more valuable than anything else you own. You don't know how much longer you're going to have to spend on the most valuable assets you have. James 4:13-14 tells us that our lives are but a "vapor or mist" that evaporates quickly. In other words, make the most out of what you've been dealt. I have a friend who is an orthopedic surgeon in the Washington D.C. area and operates on a lot of famous and wealthy present and retired Senators and Congressmen. Unfortunately, he has lost a few on the operating table replacing a knee or hip. He now asks the patients before he puts them under anesthesia what they value the most in their lives. The answer, you'd think would be their political accomplishments or wealth they have accumulated throughout the years but surprisingly, the answer is their faith, family and friends. Make each day like it's your las. Live each moment like you'll have no others. Manage your time wisely. Live your life in the next 5 minutes!

33

Effective Teaching

I'd have to say that if a lot of teachers and communicators in this world had to make a living for a week being salesmen or saleswomen, they'd starve to death. Words are symbols; we take those symbols and arrange them systematically in an order, a syntax, a grammar and we have a language as a communication tool. It's not a word message that separates the average from the excellent in communicators; it's a life message. We are all in the life business, not a word business. Our pagan society is tired of our words and hungry for reality, and they'll pack out an auditorium if they sense we have it. So communication is both verbal and nonverbal and both must be congruent [i.e.: is one wing of a plane more important than another?], what you say must correspond with what they see. Teaching that will impact is not head to head but heart to heart. In Deuteronomy 6:4-6 Moses says, "Hear, O Israel: The Lord our God, the Lord is one. Love the Lord your God with all your heart and with all your soul and with all your strength. These commandments that I give to you today are to be upon your hearts." To the Hebrews, heart embraced the total of human personality, one's intellect, emotions and will. Socrates summarized the essence of communication with three fascinating concepts that he called: ethos, pathos, and logos. Ethos spoke of character, which is what produces the learner's confidence. Pathos embraced passion and compassion. Logos claimed content or, "The meat."

Socrates thought of ethos as establishing the credibility of the teacher, his credentials. In other words, who you are is more valuable than what you say because it determines what you say and do. Who you are as a person is the greatest leverage as a speaker, a persuader, and a communicator.

Pathos or compassion addresses how the teacher arouses the passions of hearers and massages their emotions. It's your compassion that produces the listener's motivation. If I sense you care for me, I'll do all kinds of things you want me to. What kind of response do people evoke from you? Do you like people or do they bother you? Emotions must run in the same direction as do your actions. God created us all as emotional, feeling creatures so this is the secret of motivation.

Logos is what Jesus used in John 1: "In the beginning was logos, the Word. And Logos became flesh and dwelt among us, and we beheld his glory- the glory of the Father's one and only Son, full of grace and truth." When God wanted to communicate with us, he wrapped his message in a person and we as teachers are called to do the same. The logos concept therefore involves the marshaling of your evidence. It provides a reason for action and engages the minds of your listeners. The greatest communicators or teachers aren't necessarily the ones up front and highly visible. A great communicator has a great heart and they communicate as a total person. They communicate and teach to the total person of their hearers. Teaching is causing. Causes what? Causes folks to learn. All learning begins at the feeling level. People accept what they feel disposed to accept, and they reject what they feel disposed to reject. Positive attitude, the hearer will listen, negative attitude, hearer will walk away from the teaching. Good teaching has a price tag: You've got to be willing to pour out your life. In other words as Dr. Howard Hendricks says, "If you want your audience to bleed, you as the communicator must hemorrhage." Earning the right to be heard is a motto of Young Life that has made them one of the most effective youth outreach programs in the world. Be willing as a communicator to become vulnerable and transparent before those you teach, not lofty or self-exalted.

Let me conclude by giving you a spit-bath lesson and skeletal tool for preparing a teaching outline. Begin each preparation time with prayer and ask God for guidance in what He would communicate through you. Remember you're a conductor [pipe] for truth to flow not the source. Your time of speaking should begin with an introduction [a bang!]. It could begin with a clean joke, quotation, story, or a question. You want to come out of the gates with something that will grab the listener's attention and make them believe that they're not wasting their time by listening to you. Next you need to tell them what your goal during the time is and that you know what you're going to say and how to say it. In most cases, speakers can reduce the length of their message if they would known better how to say what they wanted to say [it's better to be short rather than long winded]. Organization and preparation are key and evident to the listeners if done or not done. My high school coach had a sign on his desk that read, "K.I.S.S."—Keep it simple stupid. Challenge the listeners but don't try to flatter them with your fancy words or elongated phrases. Your conclusion needs to, "Land the plane" and answer the question, "So what?" How did all this information help me today? Between the introduction and conclusion needs to be illustrations. These are windows that let in light so the hearers can say, "Aha, I see it!" Don't steal other teachers or communicators stuff [illustrations or stories], use your own. Your story is only your story and you know how to tell it best. Use visual aids if applicable and beneficial to your purpose and points. People remember only 20 percent of what they hear and 80 percent of what they see. If the audience combines what they see with what they hear, their recollection level of the material taught is higher.

A word of caution, don't answer questions ain't nobody asking. Talk in terms of where the audience is, which means you've got to know them and be sensitive to what's on their minds and hearts. When I had my 4-6pm drive-time live talk radio show in Denver and the Columbine High School tragedy happened, I needed to be informed and sensitive to how 100,000 listeners were feeling on April 20, 1999 at 11:21 a.m. A good communicator is receptor-sensitive. Speaking should be as exhausting both mentally and physically as a 10K race. Give it your all and be passionate about what you're teaching or don't teach it. So many communicators bore their listeners to death because they aren't excited about their subject matter so why should I as the hearer get excited and motivated? Your presentation involves speaking clearly so those that listen understand clearly.

Volume of your voice is another element of good communication. When you want to really emphasize something, you need to drop your level and speak softly but so the audience can hear. Don't be monotone; change your pitch throughout your message. Pick up the pace of your words when communicating something exciting; bring it down when you're emphasizing a major point.

Lastly, expressiveness through body language and facial expression are important. Look at your audience three times as much as you look at your notes. Walk around the podium and into the audience for effectiveness. The final step in communication is getting feedback. As a communicator, we all need to find out what the learners know, how they feel, and what they're doing. I need to get the listeners to tell me what they're learning verbally or by a written evaluation so I, as the communicator and teacher, can continue to refine my communicative skills. Communication is not a cakewalk and is one of the hardest and scariest things to tackle. Don't be a communicator that produces insomnia and paralyzes the audience with boredom. Pump it up!